Herreshoff Sailboats

Herreshoff Sailboats

Gregory O. Jones

First published in 2004 by MBI, an imprint of MBI Publishing Company, Galtier Plaza, Suite 200, 380 Jackson Street, St. Paul, MN 55101-3885 USA

The information in this book is true and complete to the best of our knowledge. All recommendations are made without any guarantee on the part of the author or Publisher, who also disclaim any liability incurred in connection with the use of this data or specific details.

This publication has been prepared solely by MBI Publishing Company and is not approved or licensed by any other entity. We recognize that some words, model names, and designations mentioned herein are the property of the trademark holder. We use them for identification purposes only. This is not an official publication.

MBI titles are also available at discounts in bulk quantity for industrial or sales-promotional use. For details write to Special Sales Manager at Motorbooks International Wholesalers & Distributors, Galtier Plaza, Suite 200, 380 Jackson Street, St. Paul, MN 55101-3885 USA.

ISBN 0-7603-1160-9

On the cover: *Blue Fish*, a 1916 Fish Class sloop, number 4 of 23 built by the Herreshoff Manufacturing Company in 1916. Pictured here on the St. Lawrence River, and ably handled by Martin Zonnenberg, who oversaw her restoration, *Blue Fish* was gifted to the Herreshoff Museum in 1991 by Milton Merle of New York City. The first batch of Fish Class boats, 20' 9" LOA and all gaff rigged, were built for members of the Seawanhaka Corinthian Yacht Club on Long Island Sound. *Blue Fish* is currently one of two Fish boats in the permanent collection of the Herreshoff Museum in Bristol, Rhode Island.

On the frontispiece: Close up detail of *Eleonora's* rigging.

On the title page: The schooner *Eleonora*, modelled on N.G. Herreshoff's *Westward*.

On the back cover: *(top)*Active fleets of S-boats continue to compete in New England waters over eight decades after the first was launched. *Cory Silken*

(bottom) Nathanial Greene Herreshoff (1848-1938), arguably the greatest boat designer in American history. *Herreshoff Museum*

Edited by Heather Oakley
Designed by LeAnn Kuhlmann
Photo edit by Anthony Dalton

Printed in China

Contents

Introduction

In the world of yacht design, there is no other name with the aura of Herreshoff. In response to those who produce the impressive résumés of, say, Olin Stephens or William Fife, the Herreshoff backer can produce not just the two most famous members of the Herreshoff family, Nathanael and L. Francis, but also Charles (there were four), James, Halsey, and A. Sidney deWolf.

The Herreshoffs would be worthy of a family biography on the strength of their contributions to nautical architecture alone,

but, as the pitchman says, there's more. The first American motorcycle; the sliding seat for rowboats; baking powder; an automobile; vastly improved and lighter steam engines; a deodorizer for fish oil; a vast assortment of paints, dyes, and pharmaceuticals; and a thread-tensioner for sewing machines were all products of Herreshoff genius.

The family had no greater propensity for sainthood than any other family. Genius and creativity were endemic, however, and thus there was more than the usual drama, tragedy,

Eleonora at speed. *Cory Silken*

and triumph spanning the five generations from Karl Friedrich Herreschoff's arrival in the United States a few years after our independence to the founding of the Herreshoff Museum in Bristol, Rhode Island, by Halsey Herreshoff, grandson of Nathanael.

There were fortunes made, squandered, and rebuilt. Congenital blindness cursed some members of the family to a life of darkness, and fires, fatal accidents, hurricanes, and human frailties all took their toll as this American family made its way through the generations and centuries.

There's more here than a yachting history: this is the story of a family whose journey through history carried them into contact (and marriages) with the famous, the wealthy, and the improvident. From Voltaire to the Brown family of Brown University, to Sir Thomas Lipton (he of tea and the America's Cup), to J.P. Morgan, to Aaron Burr, to John Quincy Adams, the Herreshoffs were almost always in the midst of America's dynamic growth as a world power.

And then there was the yachting business. The Herreshoff Manufacturing Company was begun in 1878 and in its heyday, the years from 1890 to 1920, so dominated the field of yacht design that the period properly became known as the "Herreshoff Era." The company's demise, beginning with the sad spectacle of the 1924 fire-sale auction of its component parts and concluding with the doors' final closing in 1945, making fact of the demise brought on by terrible 1938 hurricane, was truly the end of an era of genius.

Nathanael Herreshoff—Cap'n Nat or "The Wizard of Bristol,"—and his son, L. Francis Herreshoff, designed and built what are arguably the most beautiful, the most efficient, and the most admired sailboats that ever carved a bow wave. An unparalleled record of success in the America's Cup was the mark to which all other designers were forced to hew. They were up against the world's best designers, and pockets that were made incalculably deep by those days of no income tax backed both the Herreshoffs and their competition. From robber barons to European royalty, they all traveled to the collection of unassuming boatbuilding sheds that comprised the Herreshoff Manufacturing Company on the banks of Narragansett Bay.

It was part of the Herreshoffs' genius, though, that their best-loved boats were not

The Herreshoff Museum's waterfront at Bristol, Rhode Island. *Herreshoff Museum*

Mast and sail detail on New York 30 *Cara Mia. Cory Silken*

the graceful giants competing for international trophies but the smaller boats made for those people who wanted to sail a boat that combined beauty and function in the manner of a proper sailboat. Even to those whose knowledge of sailing vessels doesn't extend further than a pretty calendar on the wall, the beauty of a Herreshoff 12 1/2, S-class, or any of the

many classes designed for the New York Yacht Club cannot help but stir that part of the human soul which responds to hand-crafted beauty.

The timeless nature of Herreshoff designs survives today. There are well-loved originals still sailing, the pride of their owners, and many of them compete successfully against newer boats. Those new boats, some of them with the brutal looks that result from computer-aided algorithms, certainly work well, but they lack the touch of the master's hand. In fact, as a final tribute to the work of the Herreshoffs, new boats are being built to their timeless designs. These boats come down the ways built of fiberglass, aluminum, steel, ferrocement, cold-molded wood, and exotic materials that are first cousins to the space program. Lest the

ghosts of Cap'n Nat and L. Francis stir too heavily, there are also Herreshoff boats being built of wood, assembled frame by frame in sheds where boatbuilders still stand amidst aromatic heaps of curled wood shavings.

Where the yard of the Herreshoff Manufacturing Company once stood there now stands the Herreshoff Marine Museum. It is something of a temple to the art of the boat and a place for those wishing to see how genius manifests itself when confronted with the problem of turning a tree into a sculpture on the water. They made boats, the Herreshoffs, but they also made art—art that answered to the wind, agreed with the water, and brought joy to the hearts of sailors for over 100 years. The rooms where Cap'n Nat worked are still there, and his collection of hand-crafted half-models,

NYYC 40 *Rowdy* under sail.

Robert Bruce Duncan

the first step in building a boat in the days before computer-aided design, can still be touched, if you're lucky enough to be granted permission by the museum's curators. Run your hands along the hulls, feel the swell of the hull and the arc of the bow. Let your hands caress the hull as though they were water, and you will begin to see how blind John Herreshoff was

able to design a boat that fit the water as though it were a wave rather than a manmade intrusion.

Then, blessed with sight, look out the window. If it's the right day, you will see one the many Herreshoff boats that still sail their home waters. It's a sight that still inspires sailors, and it's one of the reasons this book was written.

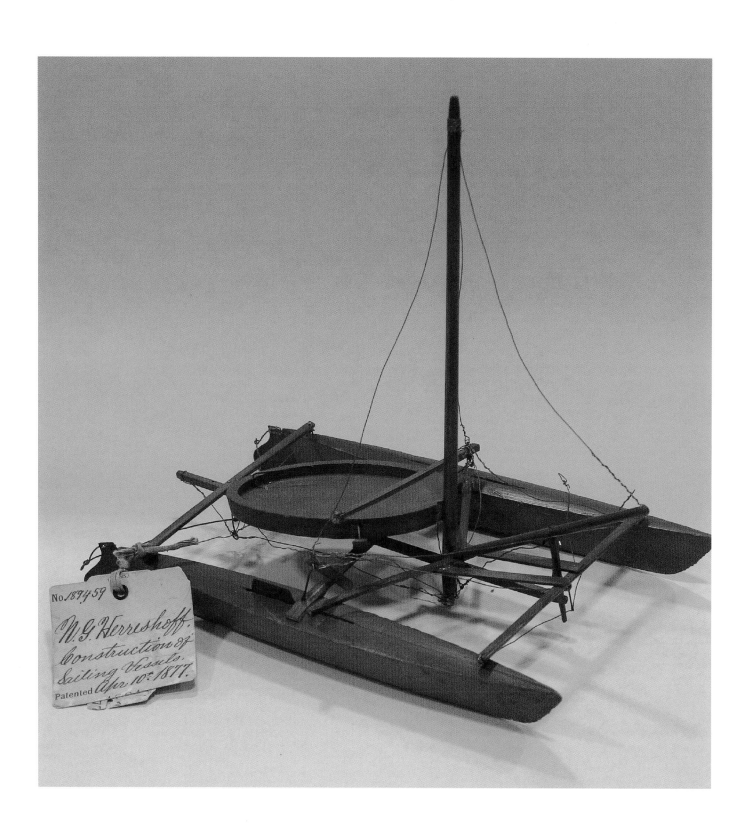

One

European Roots

T he Herreshoff family line began with what was probably a tryst between a member of Frederick the Great's
royal guard and a young woman in the town of
Minden, Westphalia, near the city of Hanover in
northern Germany.

In cases where there is some disagreement on the parent, doubt
usually centers on the identity of the father. But in the case of the
child whom we know as Karl Friedrich Herreschoff (spelling at the
time included a "c"), his father was certainly a young soldier, Corporal
Eschoff. The mother, however, was either Frau Eschoff, the corporal's
wife, or a young woman of the village named Agnes Müller.

Opposite page:

This model from 1877
depicts one of seven
catamaran designs
produced by Nat Herreshoff.
Herreshoff Museum

It is the sort of thing seemingly made for the opening chapter of a good bodice-ripping novel about the eighteenth-century Prussian military, complete with handsome, dashing soldiers and young women abandoned for the glory of the battlefield. The corporal, however, didn't live up to that scenario. Shortly after Karl Friedrich's birth on December 29, 1763, Agnes Müller died and here, too, the historic record is vague, with at least two choices as to the reason.

Corporal Eschoff, possibly regretting the whole business, and certainly filled with grief for the loss of his paramour, disappeared from history.

The chain of command in the Prussian army of the late eighteenth century was apparently a lot shorter than it is now. Frederick the

Frederick II of Prussia. *Library of Congress*

Great himself took a personal interest in young Karl, virtually adopting him at the age of five after taking what was certainly great delight in the rumors that he was the father. As he was widely rumored to be impotent, or perhaps homosexual, there is an element of humor in this; Frederick's court was composed entirely of men, and women were virtually never seen.

There was the question of a surname for the young man. The king wasn't going to make him part of the family (which would have made Karl's descendant's relatives of the British royal family, as Frederick the Great was the son of Princess Sophia-Dorothea, daughter of King George I of England). Frederick decided that Herreschoff would do nicely, combining the name of the vanished father with the prefix *Herr*, which together translates roughly as "gentleman tax assessor," or more literally as simply "Mr. Eschoff."

A recent conversation with Nathanael G. Herreshoff III suggests an alternative: *esche*, meaning "ash tree," combined with *herr* and *hof*, meaning "place of," could indicate a "gentleman from the place of ash trees." In any event, the name is unique to this family of boatbuilders, it seems, and begins with Karl Friedrich.

Young Karl became a favorite young courtier who played the flute and attended discussions of philosophy with the likes of Voltaire, also a court favorite. From all reports a tall, handsome man, Karl seemed to be on what we would call the fast track. This all changed, however, with the death of Frederick the Great in 1786 at the age of 74. Karl's wagon had been hitched to a royal star; with that star's demise, he was without a patron, and thus, like many Europeans down on their luck, he emigrated to the United States.

Karl left Europe from L'Orient, a commercial harbor on France's Brittany coast, aboard the brig *Hope*, bound for Providence, Rhode Island, with a cargo almost entirely consigned to the Brown brothers, four young men who virtually controlled the city and the colony's commercial trade. They owned a fleet of at least 40 vessels, and, in the manner of the time, engaged their fleet in everything from freelance smuggling to legitimate trade, including slaves. It is safe to say that they were among the wealthiest of the New England families.

The Browns were also patrons of the arts and education, especially when it could turn a dollar or two. In 1764, John and Moses Brown sold some of their land to the Colony of Rhode Island and Providence Plantations to establish Rhode Island College in the town of Providence. The name was changed to Brown University in 1804, the result of the family's continued financial support of the institution.

Karl arrived in New York City late in 1786, staying at a boarding house in what was then called the Bouwerie, where there lived mostly Irish and German immigrants. He was a quick study and within a few months he learned enough English to attempt, with two partners, to set up an import business. The venture was at the cusp of failure when the Brown family hired him, after an interview in Providence, as their shipping agent in New York, a job for which he was suited because of his multilingual skills.

Karl's other qualifications were the same ones that had paved the way for him in the royal court: he was tall and handsome, he played the flute, and according to those who saw him ride, had a good seat on a horse. These were the same skills and attributes that likely made him attractive to Sarah Brown, daughter of Karl's employer, John Brown.

They married after a suitably long courtship of nearly nine years and in the course of the next nine years produced six children and lived on the land that Sarah had inherited from her father, Point Pleasant Farm on Poppasquash (known in earlier years as "Papoosesquaw") Point overlooking Bristol Harbor. Karl anglicized his name to Carl Herreshoff but was notably unsuccessful as a gentleman farmer. The marriage suffered accordingly as Carl went through the money Sarah had inherited.

At the behest of Moses Brown, one of Sarah's brothers, Carl went to live on distant property the Brown family owned in the Adirondacks as the result of business dealings with Aaron Burr before the Revolution. A large, bleak piece of land, the property failed to return Carl's amateurish, if well-intentioned, efforts. After building a large mansion in which he lived, alone, he set about trying to make the land pay, trying everything from crops to sheep to, ultimately, a mine, but he only succeeded in spending money. At last, it was too much for him to bear and in 1819, just days before his 56th birthday, Carl Herreshoff killed himself with a target pistol and a well-placed shot to his head.

His widow, her inheritance nearly spent, watched Point Pleasant Farm deteriorate. The family's fortunes were somewhat revived as a result of the minor boom following the War of 1812, and her son Charles Frederick, after graduating from Brown University in 1828,

Voltaire, eighteenth-century French author and philosopher, was a contemporary of Karl Friedrich in the court of Frederick the Great. *Library of Congress*

The Middle Campus of Brown University, Providence, Rhode Island. *Library of Congress*

was able to live as a gentleman farmer at Point Pleasant. Along with puttering about the farm, building fences, hanging doors, and inventing gadgets, Charles pursued the building of small boats for his own pleasure.

Charles met and married Julia Ann Lewis, daughter of Joseph Warren Lewis and a member of one of Boston's oldest families. Her father had made more than 80 Atlantic crossings aboard boats in his fleet of commercial vessels. Julia Ann was herself a sailor, accompanying her father on pleasure cruises.

Charles and Julia married in 1833, and had nine children—seven boys and two girls—born in the course of 20 years. Nathanael Greene was the seventh child. Each child in the family was given a small sailing boat designed and built by their father and all named *Julia*, for his wife. All the children sailed competitively and often, racing against each other. This aggressive nature carried over into the sort of sibling rivalry familiar to anyone raised in a large family. During one late-night tussle in the children's bedroom, Nathanael's elder brother, John Brown, lost the sight in one eye.

The boys in the family were all clever, always conceiving ideas, contraptions, and inventions. In this they were certainly inspired by their father, who built what amounted to a lawn mower and contrived a device that used

vents of steam power to allow Julia to move cooking pots around the stove.

The children built windmills, flying toys, wind-vane steering systems for sailboats, and duck calls that were powered by the wind. Nathanael, called "Natty" in his youth, had two brothers named John: John Brown, fourth-born, and John Brown Francis, eighth in line. The elder John Brown (J. B.) built a ropewalk on the family farm, assisted by Natty. The two brothers sailed to Bristol to sell the rope, and used the money they got to buy the materials to build a boat they called *Meteor*.

Meteor was a skipjack, a low-deadrise lap-strake hull of 12 feet overall with a 5-foot beam. In the manner of the time, J. B. first built a pine model at an inch to the foot, faired it to his liking, and then transferred the lines to paper. Scaled up, the lines were then lofted life size.

Because of the increasing presence of family relatives at Point Pleasant Farm, Julia and Charles moved the family to a house on Hope Street in Bristol, also located on the bay. Julia was a teetotaler, and felt the presence of relatives, who at times were given to what she felt was an excessive fondness for alcohol, was a bad influence on her children.

The new house had a workshop for J. B., a transformed summer kitchen. Ominously, Charles built fences in the house to protect his children, as the eyesight of two of them had begun to fail.

Late one winter night in 1857, when J. B. did not return to the house after a session working on the *Meteor*, his father went out to the workshop to find J. B. in tears, the only thing his eyes could now produce—he had gone completely blind at the age of 16.

J. B. spent the winter in his room, disconsolate, but by spring, aided by his father's exhortation that there are men "who turn disaster into victory," J. B. returned to the *Meteor*, learning its curves by hand. In five weeks, assisted by his father and nine-year-old Natty, the boat was finished. On her maiden voyage, with Natty steering and J. B. trimming the main by feel, *Meteor* sailed from the Hope Street launching site to Sandy Point and back.

And how did she sail? From all reports, quite well, even though J. B. is reported to have commented she was "a little heavy on the helm. I can do better next time."

Father Charles, encouraged by his son's willpower and skill, purchased a derelict tannery across the street from the family house. He stocked it with tools and three new turning lathes, intending it to be the boatbuilding shed for J. B. and Natty. J. B.'s blindness meant the first tool he built was a walking stick with notches in it, which he used to measure his boats. J. B. whittled models, discussed ideas with Natty, and the two of them developed a mutually dependent relationship, complex in its very conception and one in which the younger Natty, the vital eyes of the operation, nonetheless very much played second fiddle.

J. B. and Natty sailed *Meteor* regularly, in between taking orders for and building small workboats for local fishermen, mostly catboats and skiffs. In the autumn of 1859 they began, in the manner of nearly every sailor, to desire a slightly bigger boat. J. B., assisted by his father, made a model of a 20-foot catboat to be named *Sprite*. At age 11 1/2, Natty took lines and measurements from the model. The result was a plumb-bowed catboat with a fine entrance and a graceful swell to the low-deadrise hull. The cockpit, surrounded by a brightwork coaming, complemented the small cuddy.

William Manchester, a local boatbuilder, initially assisted in the construction of *Sprite*. Manchester had worked with father Charles on the building of the various *Julia*s. Although he was much older than the boys, Manchester set aside his reservations about the boys' qualifica-

A Herreshoff triple-expansion steam engine from 1904. Designed to power torpedo boats, it was actually used to power generators at a Brooklyn factory. *Robert Merriam, New England Wireless & Steam Museum*

tions when he learned they were as fastidious about the boat's details as their father had been, and a May-December friendship between J. B. and Manchester developed. The apprenticeship had not yet come to fruition when Manchester died with the boat half-finished.

J. B. took up the completion of the boat, using his finely developed sense of touch and the measuring cane, while Natty, with the coming of school again in September 1859, was kept busy with schoolwork. Father Charles occasionally lent a hand but was more occupied with tending to his second son who was losing his sight, the younger Lewis, and so the bulk of the work was left to John.

By June 1860, the boat was ready and launched. The boys had heard that Isambard Brunnell's magnificent side-wheeler, the 4,000-passenger, 660-foot *Great Eastern*—the biggest ship in the world—was due to arrive in New York harbor on her maiden voyage and made plans to sail down to see her. Natty, J. B., brothers Lewis and James, and father Charles—together with an older local sailor named Georg D'Marini, on the *Sprite* and another local named Henry Slocum on *Julia* (taken on to ease their mother's worries)—set out on what turned out to be a 27-hour

Parthenia, a 130-foot steam yacht built for Morton Plant, was completed in May 1902. *Parthenia* typified Nat Herreshoff's passion for steam launches and yachts. She served as USS *Parthenia* during the last year of World War I.

National Archives

voyage. The return trip was made in 26 hours, both very creditable times.

The family curse of blindness, meanwhile, struck more of the Herreshoff children. Sister Sally lost her sight, followed by the youngest son, Julian and then Lewis, born in 1844, began to lose his eyesight as well. Julia felt somehow responsible for the family affliction, and began to spend most of her time with her sightless children, teaching them music and the then-forty-year-old written language of Braille.

There has been much speculation on the cause of the family's blindness, and for years glaucoma was blamed, but Nathanael Herreshoff III reported that there is no record of this genetically linked disease in the family. He thought the farm animals might have transmitted the blindness to the family's children. Subsequent generations of Herreshoffs have had no such problems.

Julia's devotion to her other children left Natty and J. B. with considerable free time on their hands, and the speed of *Sprite*, sailed by the two brothers in races both formal and impromptu, soon gained the boat a reputation as "easily the fastest sailer [sic] on the bay," according to Natty in his later years.

An even bigger boat followed when father Charles designed a 27-foot 6-inch catboat called *Kelpie* that the two boys built with some assistance from a Newport boatbuilder named Joe Southwick. Among the race-winning design tweaks that *Kelpie* featured was a larger version of the movable ballast that Charles had fitted on the second of the four *Julias* he designed and built. He had installed an athwartship track with a car carrying a chunk of iron weighing 550 pounds. The track had three locking positions at either end and amidships. Just before tacking, the car was released, run down to the low side, and locked in place. *Kelpie's* ballast car weighed 1,000 pounds, and the brothers discovered that half a ton of iron running back and forth in the bilge was both unwieldy and dangerous, even if it did win races.

Whatever the merits of the shifting ballast, its days were numbered. The Seawanhaka Corinthian Yacht Club, formed in 1871, made it one of its first items of business to ban movable ballasts.

In 1863, on one of *Kelpie's* first outings, J. B. and Natty took her to Martha's Vineyard to attend a camp meeting at Vineyard Haven. While there, the brothers raced *Kelpie* against a sloop called *Qui Vivre*, owned by an Englishman named Thomas Clapham, who was at the time a successful businessman residing along

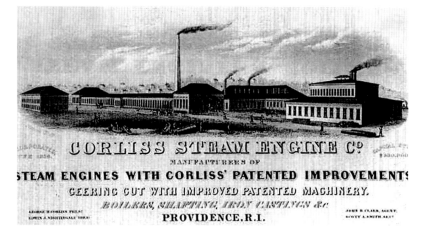

CORLISS STEAM ENGINE C?
MANUFACTURERS OF
STEAM ENGINES WITH CORLISS' PATENTED IMPROVEMENTS
GEERING CUT WITH IMPROVED PATENTED MACHINERY.
BOILERS, SHAFTING, IRON CASTINGS &c.
PROVIDENCE, R.I.

The Corliss Steam Engine Company gave Herreshoff valuable engineering experience.

New England Wireless & Steam Museum

the Housatonic River—and a man who did not like to lose sailboat races.

The first race, overseen by Rutherford Stuyvesant aboard his sloop *White Wings*, was an easy victory for *Kelpie*, as was a second race, held immediately after the first. Clapham realized the only way to beat a Herreshoff boat was in another Herreshoff boat, so he put in an order for a vessel designed by J. B. and Natty. The boat was also named *Qui Vivre* and was larger than *Kelpie*, measuring 44 feet, 11 inches LOA and 39 feet, 9 inches LWL. The beam-to-length ratio resulting from her 14 feet, 4 inches of beam was not as unusual as was the draft of only 3 feet, 3 inches. Drop the board and the draft went up to 10 feet, 6 inches. This was a boat designed for minimal wetted area, and Clapham went on to campaign her very successfully.

With this boat, the brothers, J. B. in particular, were officially in the boatbuilding business. J. B. was only 22 years old.

With the brothers building more boats, the division of labor began to make itself more apparent. Natty, much smaller than his seven-year-senior brother, was able to use his sight for the more practical aspects of boat design and construction, while J. B., being more attuned to the demands of business, took care of finances and design aspects.

The shop continued to grow; the Herreshoff brothers purchased another lathe, and Nat (the childhood nickname of Natty had become the sole provenance of his mother and he wouldn't allow anyone else to call him that), began to engage in projects of his own. When he was 16, he designed and built a small rotary steam engine with a curved condenser.

Nat's skill as a skipper also grew. Thanks to his success racing the family boats, he was soon in great demand as a racing skipper for other people's boats, but he still found time to create and design. In 1862, at the age of 14, he had made a half-model of his own design (probably his first), and in 1866, the same year he built the steam engine, he designed the catboat *Poppasquash* and a pair of 25-foot sloops, *Fanchon* and *Ariel*, both very successful on the racing circuit.

J. B.'s boatbuilding business, meanwhile, had grown to the extent that he purchased a sawmill where selected timber could be cut to his specifications. He took on several employees, and then in 1864, a partner, Dexter S. Stone. The new firm of Herreshoff & Stone

announced itself as "Yacht and Boat Builders, by steam power. Yachts and Sailboats of all sizes, built to order at short notice, with special references to SPEED, COMFORT and SAFETY, and warranted equal or superior to any others, as to style of model and construction. Also surf boats, quarter boats, schooner's yawls [*sic*], club boats and row boats, of all styles and sizes. Boat Lumber on hand for sale. Logs sawed and Lumber Planed to order."

Stone didn't last long as partner; two years later he left the partnership, with J. B. left as sole proprietor. In its April 19, 1866, edition, the *New York Tribune* published a lengthy encomium on the subject of "the Messrs. Herreshoff & Stone, the builders of the sloop *Kelpie*, which attracted so much attention at the time of the regattas last spring."

As all this was going on, Nat was increasingly isolated. J. B.'s business needed his services intermittently, and with the blindness of Sally, Lewis, and Julian, his parents were occupied with the children whom they felt needed all their energy and attention. Nat had been mulling over the design of a boat of his own, finally building a model of what was to be the 35-foot sloop *Violet*. Building the boat was a project squeezed in between the demands of John's business, and it was two years before *Violet*, built from Nat's model, was launched. The boat was entirely Nat's, from the hull to the sails, and after the launch, Nat wanted to test the boat's speed. The family practice was to test each new boat in a race against the latest *Julia*. Nat set out, father against son, evolved design versus untested, and lost the race.

The Herreshoff Manufacturing Co. would design and build all kinds of boats and ancillary equipment, such as the elegant skiff seen here and its sliding seat.
Robert Bruce Duncan

Nat was not accustomed to losing. The boat represented, to him, much more than just a design: It was the first time he had seen a boat from design to launch, and it had failed. Nathanael Herreshoff was not a good loser, and he didn't intend to get any better at it. He went back to the workshop and attacked the model with an ax, destroying it so that there would never again be another *Violet*. He didn't have the heart to destroy the boat itself, but he sold her immediately, despite his father's admonition that she was a new boat and needed a more thorough sea trial before being condemned as a design failure. Indeed, with her new owner the boat sailed another 50 years, putting silver trophies on the mantle of her owner with regularity. If Nat learned anything from *Violet*, it was that he should never judge a boat hastily. He never again destroyed a model; today, the model room at the Herreshoff Museum in Bristol, Rhode Island, has a complete set of Nat's boats, except for *Violet*.

When it came time for Nat to enroll in college, he fell out of step with the rest of the family, or at least its men, all of whom had attended Brown University. It was not the first indication of Nat's tendency to be aloof, relying upon himself for decisions and going it alone as he felt necessary. This personal bent had its beginnings in the family structure, where his blind siblings received more attention. His natural inclination to puttering and

inventing, by definition a solitary endeavor, only added to this tendency.

Enrolling at the Massachusetts Institute of Technology was a natural for Nat; the liberal arts regimen offered at Brown wasn't intended for a young man who had built a steam engine to his own design at about the same time that his peers were discovering girls and perhaps writing romantic doggerel dedicated to them.

During his freshman year at MIT in 1866 Nat attracted the attention of his analytical geometry professor during the course of a discussion on types of curves. Nat pointed out that the curve was not a new thing to him; he had used it in the design and construction of a steam engine. To silence the professor's doubts, and in response to his request, Nat had the engine shipped to MIT.

He demonstrated it before members of the university's Society of Arts, including William Rogers, MIT's first president and the principal of the School of Industrial Science. After the engine performed as Nat said it would, the assembled professors, all scientists and engineers, applauded.

This, of course, was not the beginning of Nathanael Herreshoff's infatuation with steam engines, but it certainly helped that interest along. For his entire life, even though he was known for his sailboats, Nat's steam engines and steam yachts were at least equal, in his mind, to his sailing vessels. In his later years, when his health had failed to the extent that he could no longer sail, he would go out in his steam yachts, enjoying the water no matter which boat he was on.

While studying in Boston, Nat was invited to join the Boston Yacht Club, as his brother J. B. had been. The club was founded when Nat was just 18, making him one of its earliest members. While it could be argued that he was invited to join because, as his mother's son, he was a Lewis, the club soon began to appreciate his talents. It wasn't long before he was asked to formulate a handicapping system for the members' boats in which a boat's various measurements were taken into consideration to establish a time allowance. The handicapping system used a time-for-distance calculus, quite likely the first instance of a successful handicapping system of that type. The rating system, devised in 1866, was based on waterline plus a fraction of the aft overhang (but not the bow overhang).

As happens at yacht clubs, business contacts were part of the social milieu, and Nat met George Corliss, owner of the Corliss Steam Engine Company in Providence. Corliss' engines were world famous, and in 1864 he had bought out his partners. The factory was the biggest of its kind in the world, and Nat's hiring there at the age of 21 was an early indication that his talents were already appreciated. The job offer was enough incentive for Nat to drop out of MIT after three years.

He began his career at Corliss as a draftsman but was soon promoted, spending his workdays inspecting and adjusting the giant steam engines of the day. Corliss evidently liked his young apprentice, allowing him ample time off and the freedom to set up his drawing board at work. Nat's free time was spent at his brother J. B.'s boat works, where he assisted in design, making models from John's designs and probably lending his expertise to the maintenance of the yard's steam engines. The engines were a vital part of the factory's cachet, as not many boatbuilders of that period were able to advertise that their boats were "built by steam."

Nat's visits to the boatyard were not easy. A trip from Providence to Bristol in those days involved crossing to the island by ferry, and his time was well occupied, the beginning of a life spent absorbed by work.

His first major project, in 1868, with Herreshoff Manufacturing was the design of a

60-foot steamboat, the *Annie Morse* for Samuel Shove of Pawtucket, Rhode Island. The yard found far more business designing and building steam yachts than those driven by sail, at least in larger boats. The yard built the hull of *Annie Morse*, with the engine and boiler built elsewhere.

Despite the growing emphasis on large boats, the yard's bills were mostly paid through the sale of small boats, primarily skiffs and rowboats built on a production line that was "powered by steam." Sales reached far beyond the waters of Narragansett Bay, with many of the boats exported to South America.

The shift to steamboats occurred in 1870 when J. B. built *Seven Brothers*, a fishing vessel for the Church brothers of Tiverton, Rhode Island, and *Anemone*, a launch. Both were powered by Herreshoff engines designed by Nat.

A true production line was finally set up when J. B. purchased the land next door to the old tannery, formerly the site of the Burnside Rifle Factory.

It was during this period that Nat finally had an opportunity to build a design he had been carrying in his head for some time, when he was commissioned by Dr. E. R. Sisson of New Bedford, Massachusetts, to build what would become the most successful of Nathanael's early boats and arguably one of the most important of his entire career.

J. B. also got married in 1870, to Sarah Lucas Kilton, with whom he had his only child, Katherine. Sarah and J. B. would eventually divorce, after which J. B. married Eugenida Tams Tucker in 1892.

The menhaden fishing steamer *Seven Brothers* at her owners' dock, circa 1870. Part of her job was towing the open seine boats, seen to her starboard, to and from the fishing grounds.
Herreshoff Museum

Shadow, an early centerboard gaff sloop, proved to be a consistently successful racer for over fifteen years.
Herreshoff Museum

Nat Herreshoff and his older brother, Lewis, built the 17-foot sloop *Riviera* while in the south of France in 1874 and sailed her through much of Europe on canals and rivers.
Herreshoff Museum

The 37-foot, gaff-rigged centerboard sloop *Shadow*, launched in 1871, won races beginning with her first outing, even though Dr. Sisson only raced her in a desultory fashion and sold her on to C. S. Randall, a member of the Eastern Yacht Club, after a single summer's racing. Randall went on to vigorously campaign *Shadow*, with unparalleled success.

Shadow was an evolution of two competing design styles then in vogue: the plumb-bowed English cutters and the shallow-draft catboats seen on Narragansett Bay. *Shadow* carried 10,000 pounds of ballast, and had full sections down low along the garboards. With its plumb bow, the LWL 34 feet (just 3 feet less than the overall length), and beam of 14 feet, the boat's measurements were not radical—draft was 5 feet, 4 inches with the board up—but the hull's form was truly different. The hollow in the midship section was so radical that when William P. Stephens took the lines off her in 1886 he had to use a plumb bob and a ruler to measure it.

The boat was a race winner, nearly unbeatable in years of competition. One of the few boats to ever beat her in a race was *Shona*, a G. L. Watson "extreme cutter" measuring 42 feet overall with a 33-foot-7-inch waterline, and with a beam of only 5 feet, 7 inches.

Shadow's racing successes were sufficient that the design evolved into what was called at the time a "Compromise Cutter"; that is, somewhere in between the deep, narrow English boats and the beamy, shallow American boats.

Randall owned the boat until 1873, when he sold her to Caspar Crowninshield, also a member of the Eastern Yacht Club. Crowninshield raced the boat until the end of the 1875 season, with Captain Aubrey Crocker, a well-known professional skipper, at the helm. Stephens reported that the boat was "practically invincible." Indeed, it was not until 1881, against the larger G. L. Watson boat *Madge,* measuring 46 feet overall and more than 5 feet longer on the waterline, that she lost in competition, a hotly contested two-race match in which *Madge* won the second race. *Madge,* like the aforementioned *Shona,* was an "extreme cutter," only 7 feet, 9 inches in beam and an inch less in draft.

Shadow continued to bring in silver at a steady rate, until Edward Burgess' keelboat *Papoose,* measuring 44 feet, 3 inches overall and a more sensible 12 feet, 3 inches of beam, beat *Shadow* very decisively in an open race.

This was followed by the annual Eastern Yacht Club regatta of 1886 in which *Shona* beat *Shadow* by nearly 14 minutes.

The significance of the victories, accomplished by boats not only bigger but of a completely different design, foreshadowed the design controversy that would forever change the way American yacht designers went about their craft.

As for *Shadow*'s ultimate fate, she ended her years as a commercial fishing boat, eventually burning after being abandoned as a hulk.

During this time, Nat was not a business partner in the strictest sense of the word, despite spending nearly all his free time at the Herreshoff yard. Exhausted, in 1874, family

Amarylis II, completed in 1933, was a near replica of Nat Herreshoff's original *Amarylis* from 1875, the first catamaran he designed and built. *Amarylis II* claimed a new speed record of 19.8 miles per hour in the summer of 1933.

Herreshoff Museum

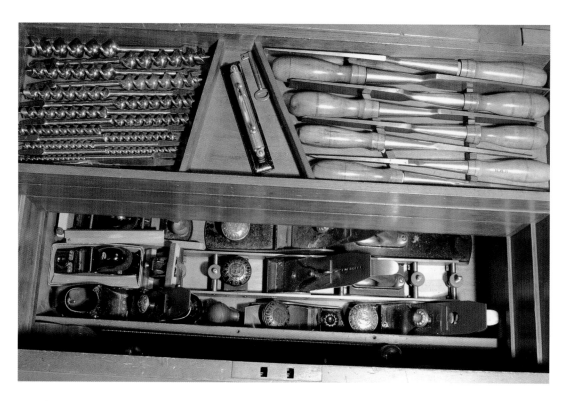

members persuaded Nat to accompany John on a trip to Europe, where they would visit Lewis, then studying music in Paris and slowly going blind.

Nat, John, and a cousin boarded the German liner *Goethe* in New York and arrived in France after a voyage in which Nat occupied himself with calculations on boat speed, propeller rpm, and visits to the engine room. They only spent a short time in Paris, heading south to Provence where they met up with their cousins, the Eaton family, living in Nice.

Nat's first order of business upon arrival was to build a boat, a small double-ender he christened *L'Onda*, which he and Lewis used to take short day sails around Nice. Desiring to explore farther, the brothers decided to build a larger boat.

Nat set to work, assisted by Lewis, in designing and building a 17-foot sloop with a shallow draft to navigate the canals of France. They built the boat, christened *Riviera*, on the city's waterfront, launching in mid-July 1874 and setting off along the coast to Marseilles. *Riviera* was sloop-rigged, with a large press of sail to accommodate the light airs. For use in canals and to make it easier to unstep the mast, Nat also designed her so that she could be rigged as a catboat.

Riviera, with her two crew, sailed to Marseilles and entered the French canal system. Via rivers and a few journeys with the boat on a railcar, *Riviera* ended up in Basel,

Switzerland, where they put the boat in the upper reaches of the Rhine River. They finally reached Rotterdam, Holland, where they put the boat on a steamer, the 3,747-ton *City of Brussels*, belonging to the Liverpool, New York and Philadelphia Steamship Company, known as the Inman Line before 1857 and as the Inman Steamship Company beginning in 1875, the year after the brothers were passengers.

When Nat returned from Europe, he went back to work for John; it was almost as if he had never left. Juggling his commitments at Corliss, where he put to good use the knowledge he gained from the busman's holiday aspect of his European trip during which he had visited every steam pumping station he could, he designed the steam engines and boilers that powered the steamboats J. B. was building.

In 1877, J. B. got his first order for a "big" boat, also his first government contract, although that wasn't immediately apparent. It was the 120-foot LOA *Estelle*, ordered by a New York lawyer who was a straw man for the Cuban government. *Estelle* was design number 39, and it should be noted that the Herreshoffs used separate systems for sail and steam. The boat was to be built as quickly as possible, and even though its construction was contracted out to Job Terry's shipyard in Fall River, Massachusetts, *Estelle* was ready in just six months.

Nat drew the lines and designed the engine and boiler. The engine was farmed out as well, to the Rhode Island Locomotive

Works, but the boiler was made at the Herreshoff works. By the end of November 1877, *Estelle* was ready for sea trials, which by any contemporary standards were a resounding success. She made a continuous speed of nearly 14 knots over a six-hour period. As soon as the boat was delivered and paid for, however, the U.S. government seized her, and she ended up her days as a tow boat in the area around New Orleans.

With his brother working on steamboats and assisted by Nat's design work, Nat continued to have sailboats on his mind. In 1875, the year after he returned from Europe, he built the 25-foot LOA *Amaryllis*, the first catamaran ever to sail in the United States. In one of those incidents of design synchronicity, in 1877, David Lazarus Davis, of Salt Lake City, Utah, launched *Cambria*, a 19-foot catamaran that featured twin rudders. There does not appear to have been any connection between the two designers, and Nat's catamaran had just one rudder in its first version.

Amaryllis first sailed with a lateen sail on a bipod mast, but Nat soon changed the rig to a more conventional jib-and-main design with a single, centrally stepped mast. After sorting out the rig, Nat entered *Amaryllis* in the Open Centennial Regatta on Long Island Sound in June 1876. His twin-hulled boat ran away from the competition, and the result should have come as no surprise: The design was outlawed as "not a yacht," thus ensuring the presence of monohull owners at the awards banquet.

Other sailors expressed their admiration, and Nat received orders for several catamarans. He took out a patent on the design, hired a few workmen, and, taking a short holiday from Corliss, went into the catamaran business. The boats sold for $750, equivalent to $12,800 today. Nat had a cat named *Tarantella* built for his own use, but the venture was not successful, and soon he was back at Corliss.

By 1878, Nat was finding it increasingly difficult to hold down two jobs and joined John as a partner in the Herreshoff Manufacturing Company, beginning a new chapter in his life and marking the true beginning of one of the most successful nautical design and construction companies in the world.

The Hall of Boats at the Herreshoff Museum contains examples of the company's boats from dinghies to steam launches.
Herreshoff Museum

Two

The Beginnings of HMC and a New Direction: The Steamboats of 1878–1900

By 1878, Nat Herreshoff, then 30, had been designing boats and steam engines for nearly half his life. With the success of *Estelle*, the 120-foot steamboat designed and built for the Cuban rebels, Nat and his brother John Brown thought it time they combined their energies and formed a business that totally involved each of them.

Nat, who seemed to have a congenital dread of debt, had some reservations about going into business with his older brother. He insisted

Opposite page:
The Herreshoff Manufacturing Co.'s buildings and docks, circa 1890. Two unidentified steam yachts can be seen. *NUWC*

that the venture, to be named the Herreshoff Manufacturing Company (HMC), should never borrow money to expand the factory or to build a boat on spec, and that the company should confine itself to building boats and engines. J. B. had run up some indebtedness with his business, and Nat was determined that once the old debts were paid, they would have no new ones.

The division of labor was made clear from the beginning. J. B. was to take care of the business end of things: preparing contracts, working up bids, and dealing with suppliers. Nat was to be the designer of both boats and engines. It is indicative of his faith in the business that he took a cut in salary of more than 30 percent to leave his position at Corliss.

New Year's Day 1878 was the Herreshoff Manufacturing Company's first day, and the brothers defined their business from the beginning. Unlike the previous business, owned and operated by J. B. and dependent on commercial and private owners for most of its business, the new company would only make boats for clients interested in and willing (not to mention able) to pay for the very best. J. B. saw military contracts as one sure source of boat orders that would be paid for and for which quality was of the highest priority. The Herreshoff Manufacturing Company was about to become the nation's leading designer and builder of fast steam yachts, and one of the best two or three in the entire world.

The formation of the new partnership marked a shift from sail to steam. Virtually

everything they built was a steamboat, because that was where the money was. Only three sailboats were built between 1878 and 1890 that were not "family projects," as the Herreshoffs became practically synonymous with steam.

The 1878 Fourth of July parade in Bristol presented an opportunity for the brothers to give public notice of the shift in the company's philosophy. They built a 30-foot LOA steam launch that they named *Waif*, a sister ship to three already built by the former business. *Waif* was set on a horse-drawn trailer and the boiler fired up. At the stern was a 27-inch-diameter propeller, square-tipped in the manner of Herreshoff props, which turned in the summer air as the boat was pulled down the street. *Waif* was design number 37, the second boat built by HMC. (The records of HMC begin in 1868 with J. B.'s Herreshoff Company.)

One of the advantages the brothers had from the very beginning was the coil-tube boiler invented in 1873 by James Brown Herreshoff, eldest of the nine and a prolific inventor. The Herreshoff Safety Coil Boiler, lighter than any of the other designs available, was also much faster producing a head of steam from a cold start.

The first coil-tube boiler was used in a steam launch named *Vision*, 40 feet overall with a 4-foot, 6-inch beam. It was designed by one of the Herreshoffs, though the record is unclear as to just which one. At that time the entire family was working together on various projects, including father Charles Frederick, son Charles Frederick (who was involved with the woodworking end of things), James Brown, and Nat. Family records indicate with fair certainty that Nat did all the working drawings, as even then this was his nearly exclusive bailiwick.

The difference in the coil-tube boiler was in the layout of its steam-producing water jacket. Conventional steam engines of the day usually had water-filled tubes running *through* the firebox, where they were heated, producing steam. The Safety Coil Boiler, however, carried the water in a coil of tubing that *surrounded* the fire and gradually increased in diameter as it went down to the firebox. This placed the water, which moved downward, closer to the fire, where it was turned to steam more quickly. The entire boiler was encased in thin sheet metal. In addition to producing steam more quickly, this system was also

The steam launch in the center is design No. 92 based on the torpedo boats of the 1880s.

Herreshoff Museum

lighter than comparable boilers. When *Estelle*, equipped with a coil-tube boiler, was being held by the revenue cutter, the crew of the cutter was compelled to keep steam up at all times, even though *Estelle's* boiler was cold: *Estelle* could make steam and pull away before the cutter could fire up her boilers and pursue the boat.

The coils, made of iron pipe, were fabricated in the Herreshoff factory and were very labor-intensive, with each coil being individually made of a tapering strip of iron, rolled into a tube, and then sealed. The Safety Coil Boiler came in two varieties, a single and a double coil. The single coil was used in boats where there were no problems with the boiler height, while the double tube allowed the boiler to be quite low and compact.

Like all good ideas, the coil-tube boiler had a palm-to-the-forehead quality to it. Water entered the smaller tubes at the top of the boiler, where the small tubes provided more surface area to be heated. After passing the length of the tubing, to the bottom of the inner coil, the steam then went to an outer coil, and then to a separator tank, where any liquid water was removed. The dry steam then went back to an upper layer of tubes where it was superheated to produce even more power.

The coil boiler was certainly efficient, although with the considerable hand labor

needed to fabricate hundreds of feet of tapered pipe it was expensive to make. Additionally, it was difficult to clean the pipes of the inevitable scale that would form inside of them and produce an insulating layer that gradually reduced both the boiler's efficiency and the amount of water inside the pipe, and affected the quantity of steam produced. The only cure was a replacement boiler but this did not, at least initially, deter its use on new designs. The coil boiler was used exclusively until some time around 1883. By then, Nat had designed boilers

Above: USS *Talbot*, sister ship to USS *Gwin*, was one of five highly successful torpedo boats built for the U.S. Navy between 1895 and 1897. *National Archives*

Left: Norfolk Navy Yard, Portsmouth, Virginia, circa 1907. Torpedo boats of the Atlantic Fleet Reserve Torpedo Flotilla. Among them are at least four Herreshoff vessels: *Dupont, Porter, Cushing*, and either *Gwin* or *Talbot*. *National Archives*

along more conventional lines, accepting the slight loss of efficiency as an acceptable trade-off for longevity.

For some customers, notably military clients, longevity was not as important as the coil boiler's other attributes. Quickly making steam was important on a military vessel, and the coil boiler's light weight made it possible for the vessel to carry a bigger payload.

"The Herreshoff steam yachts are modeled and engined for speed alone," went a report prepared by the Bureau of Steam Engineering of the U.S. Navy in 1881, "the purpose being to obtain the highest possible speed." As well as speed, the report noted "the extreme rapidity with which steam can be raised from cold water . . . the Herreshoff boiler is very greatly superior to any other known. . . . It is the safest, simplest, lightest, and cheapest, and possesses so great a balance of advantages that, in our opinion, none other can be put in competition with it."

With the engineering expertise applied to the boilers went a similar level of refinement in the engines themselves. A simple steam engine sends steam to a single cylinder, producing power as it expands. The steam is then exhausted to the atmosphere. A compound steam engine, by contrast, sends the steam from the first cylinder to a subsequent cylinder, or several subsequent cylinders. Because

some of the energy of the steam has already been used, the second cylinder is larger in bore, and the third is often larger yet. Nat's expertise, honed during his years of work at Corliss and augmented by the skilled machinists at HMC, produced what were the most efficient, lightest, and most powerful marine steam engines of the day.

The new company began with several major orders for private clients. Design number 38, a 60-foot launch christened *Puck*, hit the water in 1878, a sister ship to the previously built *Speedwell*. When a British private client ordered a steam launch as a tender for his larger vessel, the *Ibis Jr.*, with a coil boiler, was designed and built. The attractive double-ended launch was so successful HMC built two more.

The first big government order for the new company was a torpedo launch, design number 44, built for Britain's Royal Navy in 1878. Perhaps as a bit of advertising, company records indicate the boat was named *Herreshoff*. The boat was 59 feet, 6 inches LOA, with a beam of 7 feet, 6 inches. The hull and engine weighed 6 tons, and the payload of four crewmen, fuel, and two torpedoes added another 3,000 pounds. The vessel had a very shallow draft of only 30 inches, much of which was the result of the propeller, placed roughly two-thirds aft. The prop shaft was slightly curved, thus making the propeller nearly vertical in the water, in the interest of efficiency. A prop should push aft, not up, and the more a prop is angled away from vertical the greater the percentage of its thrust is used in pushing up rather than forward.

The composite hull of the torpedo launch was of wood over steel frames, with the topsides made of 1/16-inch steel plates. The engine used a coil boiler 56 inches in diameter, with some 300 feet of 3-inch pipe, roughly 30 coils, to generate steam. A 2.5-horsepower, squirrel cage–type blower (run by steam) forced the draft up the 7-foot stack. The engine was a two-cylinder compound type, with bores of 6 and 10.5 inches, with a 10-inch stroke. With a boiler pressure of only 80 psi, the propeller turned at 350 rpm, and the boat was required to show a speed of 16 knots.

The brothers were so desirous that *Herreshoff* be a success that they accompanied it, together with several other staff members, to England for its sea trials. They also took the voyage as an opportunity to deliver *Ibis Jr.* to the owner of *Ibis*, booking passage on a steamer for themselves and the two boats.

The torpedo boat was tested in the waters of the Thames River from Erith to Long Reach, a distance of about five miles. Its performance pleased the British. The boat made steam in five minutes and delivered the rated speed; moreover, with the prop fully exposed to the water, she made the same speed in reverse as forward and was able to stop dead from full speed ahead in slightly more than a boat length. The rudder, placed as far aft as possible, gave her a turning radius of roughly three boat lengths. The boat's lithe sea manners were vital for a vessel that would deliver torpedoes in a hostile environment. Self-propelled torpedoes were just coming into use and had a range of just 200 yards.

With the success of *Herreshoff*, HMC began to receive more orders for torpedo boats and soon found the physical plant of the factory was inadequate. In 1883, they built a new shop on the site of the old tannery building, especially for the construction of steam vessels. So impressive was this new, state-of-the-art facility that the magazine *Forest & Stream* paid a visit in 1885 to report on it for their readers.

Forest & Stream, founded in 1873, was one of the leading magazines of the time focusing on the outdoors. Edited by George Bird Grinnel, who also founded the Audubon Society, and

under the guidance of yachting editor C. P. Kunhardt, it gave extensive coverage to boating, covering everything from canoes to the yachts of the wealthy. Kunhardt's interest in boats was catholic; in 1887 he wrote *Steam Yachts and Launches: Their Machinery and Management*, and in 1891 wrote what some consider to be one of the finest treatises on small sailing craft of that period: *Small Yachts: Their Design and Construction*. It was not surprising that the magazine would give coverage to the new works at HMC:

> The building itself is 140 feet long and 36 feet wide, and equivalent to three stories in height. The floor is of wood, the middle portion being made in small sections. When these are removed a pit is disclosed, running down the center and into the water. This is lined with cement and fitted up with a railway for hauling and launching; the water end of the house being composed of large doors opening to the roof. A second floor is laid at the height of the eaves, on which are stored all the molds on which the vessels are built. Long windows running up almost to the roof give ample light, six steam radiators keep the building warm in all seasons, and everything is fitted to give convenience for rapid, economical and thorough work. Overhead, running on railways on the plates of the walls, are two traveling cranes, each lifting up to seven tons. On the main floor are work benches along the walls and on each side a gallery giving additional room for woodwork or getting out rigging. Outside the shiphouse are two wharves, one fitted with a powerful steam crane by which a yacht may be lifted bodily on to the dock.

It was a facility unlike anything else in the country. The big yards of Boston and New York were not "run by steam," and, unlike the Herreshoff facility, most were not expressly designed for the efficient building of boats. They had evolved, in many cases, from small one-man shops to larger facilities, and used none of the modern boatbuilding practices set up by the Herreshoffs. As a result, the competition's boats were not built with the same level of efficiency, speed, and craftsmanship as those at the Bristol yard. Herreshoff craftsmen also used power tools in greater numbers than those in other yards, and the increased production allowed J. B. to set wages that made his boatbuilders the highest paid in Rhode Island.

The naval vessel contracts were a mainstay of HMC in those years, with contracts for boats being let with regularity. In 1880, the Royal Navy stated a desire to replace their older "vedettes," small scouting boats used to report on the activities of enemy vessels and which were also armed with torpedoes, with steel-hulled boats. The Royal Navy had been using the services of a boatbuilder named John Samuel White, who operated a yard at Cowes on the Isle of Wight. His boats attained a speed of 13.3 knots, but the Admiralty wanted the new vedettes to make at least 14 knots. Bolstered by their previous success, the Herreshoffs sent a letter detailing a proposed boat that would make that speed and be lighter as well.

In June 1881, HMC built two vedettes, design numbers 74 and 75, each 48 feet LOA with an 8-foot, 10 1/2-inch beam and drawing 4 feet, 10 inches, exactly the same dimensions as White's. The Herreshoff Safety Coil Boiler powered the boats and contributed to the low weight. In the summer of 1881 HMC sent the boats to England.

After trials proved the Herreshoff boats capable of the contracted speed and then

some, turning 15.5 knots, the Admiralty decided in their favor. It wasn't a good day for the White vedette, which during the sea trials was able to turn a speed of just 12.6 knots.

The response, however, wasn't exactly what the Herreshoffs wanted: the Admiralty gave them an order for two smaller boats, a pair of 33-foot LOA open launches, design numbers 80 and 81. J. B. was desirous that his boats do their best, and so in October 1881, accompanied by his ten-year-old daughter Katherine, delivered the boats to the banks of the Solent for sea trials.

Once again the Herreshoff boats were pitted against White boats, and the Safety Coil Boiler, coupled with the light weight and fair lines of the HMC designs, drove the Herreshoff boats to a trials speed of 9.25 knots, while the White launch was able to make only 7.3 knots.

The Admiralty was impressed, and in a break with their usual policy of paying bills as slowly as possible, sometimes even "forgetting" to pay, they terminated the sea trials after the speed tests and paid J. B. for his boats in the space of 10 days.

During this period, civilian work was not ignored, of course, and one of the largest boats

The 1876 spar torpedo boat *Lightning*, first torpedo boat for the U.S. Navy, off Newport. Unlike today's self-propelled torpedoes, *Lightning*'s torpedoes were set out at the end of long poles and dropped beside enemy ships. The torpedo boat then had to back away rapidly to avoid being caught in the ensuing explosion. *Herreshoff Museum*

made in the early years of HMC was the 112-foot LOA steam yacht *Gleam*, design number 65, built in 1880 for William Graham, a regular customer at the Herreshoff yard. He traded in the 100-foot steam yacht *Leila*, design number 40, also a Herreshoff boat, in partial payment for *Gleam*, and the Herreshoffs made good use of *Leila*. They put a crew aboard, paid all the bills, and lent the boat for sea trials to the U.S. Navy, whose serious interest in Herreshoff boats went back at least as far as 1876 when they purchased the 57-foot spar torpedo boat *Lightning*, design number 20. The Navy put *Leila* through lengthy trials. It's not inconceivable that an admiral or two who enjoyed the speed and comfort of a private yacht while testing boats for the Navy made day trips aboard *Leila*.

When the Navy wrote its glowing report on the Herreshoff boats quoted above, it was *Leila* they were talking about, after the two-year test program. *Leila* was sold in 1882 to an owner on the Great Lakes, but before she left, her auxiliary two-masted sail rig was removed and one of the masts became the flagpole in front of Nat's house.

Gleam was similarly rigged, looking like a schooner with a large wheelhouse forward of the foremast. The large stack of the steam plant emerged nearly vertically and roughly equidistant between the masts, which had low booms for the auxiliary sails. She was designed with a nearly plumb bow, most of the 10 feet of overhang being drawn into the stern. With a beam of 15 feet, 3 inches and a draft of 6 feet, 7 inches, she was of the slender hull shape used in steam vessels of the era.

Gleam had a two-cylinder compound engine, with bores of 10.5 and 18 inches with an 18-inch stroke, and the Safety Coil Boiler was 5 feet, 6 inches in diameter.

Gleam was built, as were most of the new steam yachts, in the new boatshop called the "South Construction Shop," which, besides its orientation, was distinguished from the North Construction Shop by having a marine railway. The North Shop featured the traditional means of launching: both it and the South Shop extended out from the shore, which was across the street from the rest of the facilities, and had a wharf.

Magnolia, a 99-foot twin-screw steam yacht, with a light schooner rig, was built for Fairman Rogers of Philadelphia in 1883. *Herreshoff Museum*

⊰STILETTO⊱

When the Herreshoff's personal steam yacht, *Stiletto*, beat the great passenger steamer *Mary Powell* in an 1885 race, the Herreshoff Manufacturing Co.'s name became known nationwide, and was front-page news in New York papers. *Herreshoff Museum*

Out of the new South Shop was to come a steady procession of steam vessels, usually of composite construction comprising steel frames and wood planking. Some of the more outstanding of the private yachts built include the cabin launch *Edith*, 60 feet overall and 55 feet LWL, 9 feet, 2 inches beam and drawing 3 feet, 5 inches. *Edith*, design number 77, was built for a New York yachtsman named William Woodward Jr. and had a two-cylinder compound engine with bores of 6 and 10.5 inches and a stroke of 10 inches.

In June 1882, HMC built design number 88, the steam launch *Siesta*, 98 feet LOA, for H. H. Warner of Rochester, New York, who had made his fortune selling patent medicines. Also that year, in July, HMC built *Permelia I*, design number 92, a 95-foot LOA steam yacht with a two-cylinder compound engine with bores of 8 and 14 inches and a stroke of 14 inches. *Permelia I* was built for Mark Hopkins of Port Huron, Michigan, the treasurer of the Hopkins Steamship Company.

Hopkins liked *Permelia I* so much that he ordered another, *Permelia II*, built in 1883 and 5 feet longer overall with a waterline of 94 feet, a beam of 12 feet, 6 inches, and a draft of 5 feet, 9 inches. *Permelia II* was design number 100 for HMC, and among her features was an auxiliary schooner rig that used sail tracks, rather than parrels, to rig the sails. It was invented by Nat and built in the yard. *Permelia II*'s two-cylinder compound engine, with bores of 12 and 21 inches and a stroke of 12 inches, was unusual in that steam was made in a Hazelton boiler, a vertical-tube boiler more often found in stationary engines.

Permelia I was eventually sold, renamed *Aida*, and developed a certain fame, if not notoriety, for the new owner's choice of paint for the boat, a color described charitably as "royal blue" and possibly with more accuracy as just plain "purple." In the late nineteenth century, the acceptable pallet for boats was black and white, usually with a black hull and white topsides and sometimes

USS *Stiletto* firing a torpedo from a single bow tube. Originally a steam yacht, *Stiletto* was converted at the Bristol shops and sold to the U.S. Navy in May 1888 as an experimental torpedo boat. *NUWC*

a white hull as well. Any other color was virtually unheard of.

The biggest boat yet built by HMC, in 1882, was the *Orienta*, design number 89, at 126 feet, with a large two-cylinder compound engine measuring 14 and 24 inches in bore with a 24-inch stroke. *Orienta* was built for Jabez Bostwick of New York City, the purchasing agent for the Standard Oil Trust. Among his other duties was setting the daily price for petroleum from his offices. It is also significant that he later became involved with the manufacture of naphtha engines, which were to briefly challenge the steam engine for supremacy in the marine propulsion field.

Orienta was too big for the existing boathouse, and was instead built outside. Undertaking a project of this magnitude with the boat exposed to the vagaries of New England weather certainly gave some impetus to the decision to build the South Shop boathouse.

In 1883, the Herreshoff brothers broke new nautical ground with the design and construction of a unique boat for a unique client: the 99-foot LOA, 17-foot, 6-inch beam and 4-foot, 3-inch draft vessel named *Magnolia*, design number 104. The beam, verging on extreme in those days, suited the owner, Fairman Rogers, very well.

One of the wonderful aspects of yachting in the years surrounding the turn of the twentieth century was that, in a country still fairly small in population, the number of influential people was also small and they tended to be connected to each other in surprising ways. Money, of course, was the common denominator, and the "robber barons" —industrialists, inventors, and merchants who were transforming the nation's industrial and financial landscapes—were also, in many cases, involved with the advancement of the arts.

Rogers was no exception. The son of a wealthy industrialist and a professor of civil engineering at the University of Pennsylvania, he was one of the original members of the National Academy of Sciences and also had a deep and abiding interest in fine arts. A chairman of the Committee of Instruction at the Pennsylvania Academy of Fine Arts, Rogers worked closely with painter Thomas Eakins and, as an enthusiastic amateur photographer, asserted some influence on the work of Eadweard Muybridge, famed for his early motion studies using photography.

Rogers' varied interests and wide range of friendships were facilitated, no doubt, by the

ownership of a boat that was more than a trophy or an emblem of success. He needed a boat that could be used for travel, living abroad, entertaining friends, and conferring with the artists, painters, and photographers for whom he was a patron. The result of these needs was, for all practical purposes, the first houseboat.

Magnolia was a twin-engine, twin-screw vessel, with each engine measuring 6 and 10 1/2 inches bore, respectively, with a 10-inch stroke. The engines had Safety Tube Boilers with blower-assisted draft. Rogers sailed his boat as far as the West Indies and the length of the East Coast. *Magnolia* was rigged as a gaff schooner in the manner of many of the steam yachts, but her design was distinctive in several ways, largely due to the desires of the client. To provide greater living space below, her freeboard was much higher than nearly anything of her size and purpose then on the water. The increase in freeboard allowed *Magnolia* to be virtually flush-decked while still providing full headroom below and a draft sufficiently shallow for Rogers to enjoy cruising in the Caribbean.

Newspaper mogul William Randolph Hearst was just one of Herreshoff Manufacturing Co.'s influential clients.
Library of Congress

Hearst's Herreshoff–designed and built 112-foot steam yacht, *Vamoose*, was said to be the fastest of its type in America when it was first in service.

Library of Congress

Despite *Magnolia's* freeboard, she maintained a rather elegant air. Her masts and the funnel were raked aft at 8 degrees, contrasting nicely with her nearly vertical bow. Her stern overhang was very modest as well, providing ample interior volume.

Also built in 1882 was design number 83, the 76-foot LOA steam yacht *Nereid*, for Jay C. Smith of New York City, as well as *Sport* and *Lucy*, the first in a series of launches especially as tenders to large sailing yachts. To give some perspective on scale, *Sport* and *Lucy* were 45 and 42 feet LOA, respectively.

While HMC was designing and building boats for private clients, their work for military clients was taking up increasing amounts of time. The work may be said to have truly begun in 1876 with the building of the spar torpedo boat *Lightning* for the U.S. Navy, but after the start of the Herreshoff Manufacturing Company in 1878, military contracts became increasingly important.

J. B. and Nat understood the value of publicity, and in the late nineteenth century, the nation was obsessed with speed. A steamboat could travel nearly as fast as a steam train, and the operators of both steamboats and trains were popular heroes.

Other yards and designers were making fast steamboats. It was the technology of the day, the very essence of modernity, and the field was quite competitive. In 1861, the 260-foot side-wheeler *Mary Powell* was launched from a yard in Jersey City, New Jersey, built to the design of her owner, Captain Absalom Anderson. He returned the following year to have 40 feet added to her. At 300 feet, she was reputed to be the fastest vessel of that length anywhere in the world. Her legendary speed made her a benchmark for other boats, and when Nat designed and built the 94-foot LOA *Stiletto* in 1885, he and J. B. had one goal in mind: speed. They wanted *Stiletto*, and by extension, HMC, to be known for the speed of their boats. The surest way to do this would be to challenge *Mary Powell* to a race.

The boats couldn't have been more different. *Mary Powell* had a beam of 34 feet, 6 inches and drew 10 feet 4 inches. Her twin side-wheels were 31 feet in diameter. *Stiletto*, design number 118, was just 94 feet long, with a beam of 11 feet and a draft of 7 feet, 10 inches. She was driven by a screw propeller of Herreshoff design and manufacture, a massive four-bladed affair 4 feet in diameter. At full speed, it turned at 400 rpm, with a pitch of 80 inches.

Stiletto was built long and narrow, of composite construction, like the other steam yachts, but with a propulsion system designed

USS *Cushing* at speed. An 1890 torpedo boat, *Cushing* was powered by two large five-cylinder quadruple-expansion engines. On her speed trials she reached 26 miles per hour.

National Archives

for speed. The engine was a two-cylinder inverted compound with bores of 12.6 and 21 inches and 12-inch stroke. Steam was made in a 7-foot square sectional water-tube boiler running at 160 psi.

While *Mary Powell* was a fairly standard passenger boat, with three decks, a massive pilothouse, and deck space for cargo or passengers, *Stiletto* was unusual in nearly every respect. Built with considerable tumblehome to her and reverse sheer, with a large wheelhouse and three masts, raked aft at 8 degrees, she was not likely to be confused with any other vessel. Breaking with a financial practice that had served HMC well since its inception, *Stiletto* was not built for a customer. She was built as an advertisement that the boats from the Herreshoff Manufacturing Company were the fastest in the world.

The June 10, 1885, race was an important event. *Mary Powell* would have on board nearly everyone involved in the steamboat business, and all eyes would be on the little boat. An indication of the importance the Herreshoffs placed on the race can be judged from the crew list of that day. Leading the Herreshoff clan was father Charles, 74 years old, with four of his sons, James Brown, John Brown (J. B.), Nat, and youngest of the brothers, John Brown Francis, all together with an HMC employee known to us only as "Gray," who was the fireman.

All the newspapers of New York City covered the race, with reporters both on board the *Mary Powell* and at various places along the shore. The *New York Morning Journal's* shore-side reporter at the start of the race, just across from the 23rd Street pier, wrote:

> Jing-aling-ling, sounded *Stiletto's* bells, and with almost a bound she leaped forward. But *Mary Powell* was going very fast and crept up and up on *Stiletto*. It was a moment of intense excitement. Like the *Prairie Belle* on the Mississippi, the *Powell* had never been passed. Brave old Captain Anderson, whose pet she was for years, was not on board or his heart would have warmed to this last word of science dropping back from his lovely queen. Cheers break out from the passengers on board the *Powell* and handkerchiefs are waved.

As the race progressed *Stiletto* slowly gained on *Mary Powell*. Contemporary reports from aboard the bigger boat state that *Stiletto*, when alongside, rang her bell again and those aboard *Stiletto* greeted the passengers with a cheery "Good afternoon, gentlemen," before pulling slowly ahead.

Sing Sing was the first scheduled stop, 30 miles up the Hudson from the start, and *Stiletto* arrived five minutes ahead of her rival, with an elapsed time of one hour, 15 minutes. By comparison, the express train from New York City took one hour and two minutes to cover the same route.

The victory was sweet for the Herreshoffs. They had proved to the world that they made the world's fastest steamboats, and in 1887 the U.S. Navy was at the factory door. They bought *Stiletto* for use as a torpedo boat, commissioning the HMC yard to reduce the size of the pilothouse and add a forward-firing torpedo tube on the starboard side of the bows.

Private clients, the moneyed class interested in buying the best and fastest, were also at the door. Norman L. Munro, who had made his fortune publishing sensational potboilers, the "dime novels" that were a mainstay of popular fiction, ordered *Henrietta*, a 48-foot launch, in 1886. With his new boat and its triple-expansion engine (measuring 4 x 6 1/2 x10 inches with an 8-inch stroke), one of five produced on the same lines, he proceeded to challenge most of the commercial steamboats known for their speed. *Henrietta*, design number 133, looked like a traditional Whitehall rowing boat, with a wineglass transom and a long,

graceful sheer line, but longer, and soon Munro was back, wanting a larger, faster boat.

He commissioned *Now Then*, design number 142, in 1887, 84 feet overall, 81 feet on the waterline, with a beam of 10 feet and drawing 2 feet, 6 inches. Munro specified the shallow draft to accommodate the water at his home on the Shrewsbury River. The design represented a change in thought for Nat. Gone was the aft overhang and in its place was a reverse transom, described by contemporary viewers as a "duck's bill." This was done to reduce the squatting at the stern evidenced by his previous boats when they were at speed, for it was speed that dictated *Now Then's* lines.

The stern design of *Now Then* was only used on this particular boat. In the memoirs published by Nat's son, L. Francis, he notes that when the boat was backing out of a slip, waves were carried up on deck by the reversed transom and soaked several women on the afterdeck, one of whom was Nat's mother.

The engine was a triple-compound of 7.5, 12, and 19 inches, with a stroke of 10.5 inches, connected to the four-bladed, 36-inch prop by a massive shaft of 3.25-inch diameter.

And the boat *was* fast. Munro offered to race any boat in the country—and to give a 10-mile head start. On her maiden voyage, *Now Then* made a run from Bristol to New York City, 130 miles distance, in seven hours, four minutes, averaging just over 18 mph.

The search for speed is a demanding mistress, however, and Munro was back in 1888.

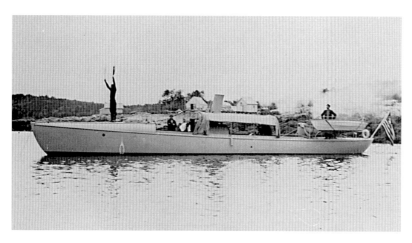

Above: The steam launch *Mist* as a private vessel early in the 1900s. In April 1917 she was commissioned into the navy as USS *Mist*. *National Archives*

Right: In contrast to the smaller steam yachts measuring between 48 and 65 feet, *Ballymena* stretched an impressive 145 feet from bow to stern. She was completed in 1888. *Herreshoff Museum*

The result was the 132-foot *Say When*, design number 150, with a more conventional stern profile.

Say When had a five-cylinder, quadruple-expansion engine, with bores of 11 1/4, 16, and 22 1/2 inches, with a stroke of 15 inches, developing roughly 875 horsepower. HMC guaranteed a speed of nearly 22 knots, pushed by a 52-inch-diameter propeller with a 100-inch pitch.

On her sea trials, skippered by Nat, *Say When* failed to make the speed he thought she was capable of when the safety valve opened and dropped the boiler pressure before she got up to speed. As Nat was getting pressure back up for another run, a boiler tube burst while the fire door was open, and the exploding steam killed the fireman. Boiler-tube ruptures were not that uncommon, and often boats continued on their way, making port before running out of water. As skipper and as a licensed steam engineer, however, Nat was held responsible for the tragedy, and an investigation resulted in a reprimand. Nat's steam engine license was permanently revoked. If there is a single event that can be said to have initiated the shift of HMC from steam to sail it was this. Nat could continue to design steam engines, but he couldn't operate a steam engine on a seagoing vessel.

HMC continued on in the lucrative steam yacht business. There were only a few good years left, but what years they were.

In July 1890, William Randolph Hearst of newspaper fame and fortune placed an order for the 98-foot *Javelin*, design number 164, 94 feet on the waterline with a 10-foot, 2-inch beam and drawing 4 feet, 9 inches. The boat wasn't even completed when Hearst changed his mind and ordered a bigger boat, design number 168, to be called *Vamoose*, measuring 112 feet, 6 inches LOA; 100 feet, 4 inches LWL; 12 feet, 4 inches beam; and drawing nearly 7 feet. But *Javelin* wasn't to be homeless. When Hearst decided he would rather have the bigger *Vamoose*, *Javelin* was bought, partially completed, by E. D. Morgan in January 1891. Morgan was also something of a "regular" who had purchased two other sailing vessels, including the famous 46-foot sloop *Gloriana*, at roughly the same time.

Vamoose used the quadruple-expansion engine design that had been used on *Say When*, whereas *Javelin* had a triple-expansion engine of 9, 14, and 22 1/2 inches bore with a 12-inch stroke and was guaranteed by HMC to make a speed of 20 knots. She managed over 22 knots in trials and in races.

Vamoose and *Javelin* took on *Mary Powell*, soundly defeating the old girl, and then proceeded to race against other fast commercial steamboats, defeating them as well. Both *Javelin* and *Vamoose* looked like steamboats, with no evidence of auxiliary masts. Although

J. B. Herreshoff's personal yacht, *Eugenia I*, steaming sedately past a fin-keel Newport 30 sloop, both classic examples of nineteenth-century Herreshoff designs.
Herreshoff Museum

The steam yacht *Scout* was one of many Herreshoff steam yachts acquired by the U.S. Navy during World War I. She is seen here as a civilian vessel. *National Archives*

it would stretch the definition to say either of the boats was pretty, they had a purposeful look, with not much more than a pilothouse on deck and open seating aft of the raked funnel.

Hearst's *Vamoose* was reputed to be the fastest steam yacht in the world, a spare racehorse of a boat that spent her short time on the East Coast occupied in a search for boats to race against. After less than a year, she was put aboard a freighter and shipped to the West Coast.

As the century neared its close, military construction occupied HMC as well. In 1888,

the yard entered a contract with the U.S. Navy for a torpedo boat, 138 feet long and 134 feet at the waterline. With a beam of 15 feet, drawing 4 feet, 8 inches, and a displacement of roughly 100 tons, two five-cylinder, 1,000-horsepower engines had to push the boat at least 22 knots. For every 1/4 knot over that, a bonus of $1,500 would be added to the contracted price of $82,750 (just over $1.5 million today); for every 1/4 knot over 24 knots, a bonus of $2,000 would be paid. If the boat couldn't make 22 knots, a penalty of $4,000 would be charged, and if the boat couldn't make at least 20 knots the Navy could reject the contract.

The boat was design number 152, the *Cushing*, powered by a pair of the same quadruple-expansion steam engines used on *Say When* and *Vamoose*. *Cushing* wasn't much faster than *Stiletto*, despite having two engines. She was certainly heavier, having been built of galvanized steel, and the twin screws had more driving force, but her absolute speed was reckoned from sea trials to have been just under 23 knots.

On the commercial side, Munro's taste for Herreshoff yachts was seemingly insatiable.

The Herreshoff Manufacturing Co.'s first property on Burnside Street in Bristol, Rhode Island, stands beyond J. B. Herreshoff's home. *Herreshoff Museum*

He also commissioned *Lotus Seeker*, at 48 feet; *Jersey Lily*, 65 feet; and *Our Mary*, 65 feet; the latter two named after famous actresses of the time, Lily Langtry and Mary Anderson. *Jersey Lily* and *Our Mary* were put into service as passenger launches on the Shrewsbury River.

The massive five-cylinder engine would power one more boat, the biggest ever designed by Nat: the 145-foot *Ballymena*, in 1888. Design number 151, she was the first all-steel yacht built by HMC, and a departure from most of the previous boats in that the boiler was not a Herreshoff Safety Coil but a water-tube type built by the Almy Water Tube Boiler Company in Providence, Rhode Island. *Ballymena* was, like all of Herreshoff's boats, fast, although speed was less of a factor with this boat than was comfort. She was built for Alexander Brown of Baltimore, whose father of the same name had immigrated to this country in 1800 from Ireland and founded the Baltimore & Ohio Railroad and owned a fleet of cargo ships. The son named his vessel after the town his father left in Ireland. Her dimensions were not out of the ordinary; with a beam of 18 feet she was typically narrow, although her draft of 11 feet, 6 inches was fairly deep. In 1893, she had a recorded passage of 168 miles

in 10 hours and 55 minutes, or nearly 13 1/2 knots, not in the speed range of *Vamoose*, *Stiletto*, or *Cushing*, but she was a luxurious yacht, with full accommodations. She displaced 145 tons, carried a gaff-schooner auxiliary sail rig, and had a graceful clipper bow.

The final years of the nineteenth century were truly glory years for HMC's steam yacht business. They built boats for the rich, the powerful, and the navies of the world. A roster of the most prominent steamboats built from 1888 onward hints at their range of projects: 1889: *Augusta* (131 feet); 1890: *Katrina I* (73 feet), *Judy* (102 feet), *Reposo* (72 feet); 1892: *Truant* (132 feet), *Tranquilo* (80 feet); 1893: *Louisa* (102 feet), *Kaloah* (92 feet); 1894: *Eugenia I* (75 feet), *Neckan* (100 feet); 1895: *Eugenia II* (86 feet); 1896: *Vacuna* (84 feet); 1897: *Katrina II* (100 feet), *Nina* (99 feet); 1898: *Squib* (65 feet and built for Nat); 1900: *Florence* (98 feet), *Mirage* (81 feet), and *Scout* (80 feet). Later, well into the twentieth century, HMC continued the steady design and building of fast, big, custom steam yachts. But there was a new wind blowing at HMC and it would bring with it the boats they are best remembered for, and for which the Herreshoff family is world famous: their magnificent sailing vessels.

Herreshoff Manufacturing Co.'s employees, such as this shop crew from 1882, worked six days a week from 7:00 a.m. to 6:00 p.m. Many worked for Herreshoff Manufacturing Co. from youth to old age.
Herreshoff Museum

Three

The Sailing Vessels of 1878–1900

With the formation of the Herreshoff Manufacturing Company, Nat and J. B. set out, very deliberately, to make the best possible boats, with no compromise in quality, and to court only those buyers who could afford and wanted the very best.

As noted in Chapter 2, the brothers initially concentrated on steamboats, but in the closing years of the nineteenth century they also built sailing vessels. In fact, by the end of the century, they had become more famous for their sailboats than for their steamboats, a remarkable achievement, considering the reputation they had built in steam. Some of the sailboats built at HMC in those years were built

Opposite page:

Wasp, a 46-foot–class sloop, was launched in 1892 and proved a worthy successor to *Gloriana*. *Library of Congress*

for the Herreshoffs. Often these were boats with unique or novel design characteristics, and served as test beds for designs which, if successful, were incorporated into boats built for paying clients. One such a boat was the cat yawl *Consuelo*, design number 400 (HMC's sailboat construction record began in 1883, and the first design was given the number "400," as at that time the steam yacht side was at design number 100). *Consuelo* was built in 1883 for Nat to his specifications. In the first years of HMC, Nat was often seen sailing his catamarans, but when he married Clara Ann DeWolf in 1883, he needed a more comfortable boat on which to take his new wife out for day sails in Narragansett Bay. This was one reason why he designed *Consuelo*.

Consuelo was 32 feet overall, 28 feet, 6 inches on the waterline, and 8 feet, 8 inches beam. One contemporary observer described her cat yawl rig as "novel." With her fixed keel—which was something of a surprise, given Nat's well-known fondness for centerboard yachts—*Consuelo* drew 5 feet, 8 inches. The mizzen was diminutive, even for a yawl, just enough to balance the mainsail. Both sails were fully battened, and a diagonal batten served the function of a gaff, allowing the sail to be set with a single halyard. The mizzen had a small sprit rigged from the mast to the end of the boom, looking something like a proto-wishbone rig. It served to reduce the tendency of the boom to lift when off the wind, and versions of this on headsails, mains, or mizzens would show up on Herreshoff boats for the next 50 years.

The one design feature that stood out most clearly on *Consuelo*, however, was the steering arrangement. A vertical rod with a crossbar at the top and a hand-sized vertical rod at each end was visible above deck. As the helmsman rotated the crossbar as though he were cranking open the gate of a lock, a pinion gear at the bottom of the vertical shaft engaged a rack with vertically cut gears attached to the rudderstock that turned the rudder. It was neat, effective, simple, and long lasting. It also had about as much nautical flavor as the braking controls on a streetcar, which it strongly resembled, and this particular design exercise was only seen on *Consuelo*. Also unique to the boat was a folding top, which when folded down resembled a convertible top on an automobile. The top was held up by roof bows of steamed and bent wood. When the top was up, it looked like a short, seagoing version of a Conestoga wagon. This, too, was a design feature with a short life.

Nat sailed *Consuelo* from 1883 to 1886, when he sold her to Pierre Lorillard, one of the yard's regular clients. Lorillard took such a fancy to Nat's boat that he was eventually able to persuade him to part with the unique yawl. Nat nearly always had a sailboat for his personal use, even though his working habits included six- or seven-day work weeks. Even in midwinter he would go for short day sails aboard one of the open, unballasted boats he favored.

After selling *Consuelo*, Nat designed and had built *Clara*, another cat yawl, 36 feet overall and 29 feet, 3 inches on the waterline. She was 9 feet, 10 inches at maximum beam and drew 5 feet, 5 inches. Much like her predecessor, both sails were fully battened and the upper mainsail batten served as the gaff boom. *Clara*, design number 402 and built in 1887, had a nearly plumb bow and impeccable seagoing manners.

Following *Clara*, Nat designed *Coquina*, design number 404, in November 1889. A

Nat at the helm of his cat yawl *Clara*. She was similar in hull design to the superb pilot cutters developed in Britain around the same time. *Herreshoff Museum*

Nat Herreshoff's personal sailboats, the cat yawls *Clara* and *Coquina*, circa 1890—the former a fixed keel and the latter, half *Clara*'s size, a centerboard. *Herreshoff Museum*

centerboard cat yawl measuring 15 feet 9 inches LWL with a beam of 6 feet and drawing 15 inches with the board up, she was one of his all-time favorites. He sailed her year-round, sometimes by himself and sometimes with his family aboard for day trips to nearby islands for picnics. *Coquina* stayed in the Herreshoff family until destroyed in the disastrous 1938 hurricane.

In 1890, Edwin D. Morgan, one of HMC's regular clients, paid a visit to Bristol to talk boats, probably discussing at some length the rather disappointing racing record of his steel-hulled, 40-foot class Burgess-designed *Moccasin*. Upon finishing their discussions, Nat offered to take Morgan down the bay aboard *Clara*, in company with *Moccasin*. When Morgan took the helm, he was surprised to see how easily *Clara* kept up with *Moccasin*, some 10 feet longer on the waterline. The experience was enough that he was soon back in Bristol ordering a 27-foot steam launch for himself and a *Clara*-based cat yawl for his brother-in-law, Percy F. Moran. The yawl was to be named *Pelican* and modified to the extent that it incorporated a fish well and was slightly shorter, at 26 feet, 6 inches, with a commensurately narrower beam of 9 feet, 1 inch. That same day, E. D. Morgan ordered another nearly identical cat yawl for himself, which he christened *Gannett*, design number

Gloriana, seen in a Goelet Cup Race, was launched for E. D. Morgan in 1891. That summer the 46-foot–class sloop entered and won eight races. *Library of Congress*

408, drawing 5 feet, 11 inches like *Pelican*. He paid $3,000 for each of the boats, or about $60,000 each today.

Morgan's pleasure in Nat's boats was critical in the history of HMC. In 1890, Morgan was on a train with Royal Phelps Carroll of Baltimore, who told Morgan of his plans to have a boat built to compete in the 46-foot class. Morgan, having just finished his visit to the Herreshoff yard, advised Carroll to have the work done by Nat.

Carroll took Morgan's advice. However, after signing a contract and with work about to begin, Carroll's love life took a turn for the better and he made plans to be married. He wrote to Nat, saying he wasn't sure about indulging simultaneously in both marriage and a yacht, and asked the cost of breaking his contract. The Herreshoff brothers replied with a letter of congratulations and the welcome news that they would not charge him anything for releasing him from the contract. The factory had plenty of work, and so the Carroll boat was set aside. Nat had made a model, taken lines off it, and was ready to build the

boat, but other vessels with guaranteed owners took precedence.

In February 1891, E. D. Morgan was back at the Bristol works, and in the course of looking around came across the Carroll boat. He liked the looks of the model, inspected the plans, and decided that it would be his next purchase. He named her *Gloriana*, after the queen of the land of Faerie in Edmund Spenser's allegorical poem, "The Faerie Queene." *Gloriana* represented a major change at HMC, where in the 12 years since its founding, the works had only made 10 sailboats, four of them for family members, and all of them under 30 feet on the waterline. *Gloriana*, design number 411, was more than just a bigger boat—she was the embodiment of all that Nat had learned about sailboat design and, more importantly, construction, in his life so far. She was built, as were many of the other 46-foot class boats, of composite construction, with steel frames and wood planking. But whereas many of the boats built in other yards had problems with leaky planking, *Gloriana* was built to a higher standard. Nat overbuilt the frames, making them 1 3/4 inches square and spacing them at 16-inch centers. The entire hull, as well as the deck, was strapped diagonally, and below the waterline the planking was a single layer of 1 3/8-inch yellow pine. Above the waterline she was double-planked with 1/2-inch white cedar covered by 7/8-inch yellow pine. The planks were held to the frame with bronze bolts and the two layers were held together with brass screws.

The use of brass screws rather than copper rivets to attach planking was one of Nat's ideas, an innovation that seems so sensible in retrospect that it's hard to imagine there was a time when boats weren't assembled with screws. But that wasn't Nat's only construction innovation. Nearly every aspect of building a hull is simplified if the boat is upside down in its early stages, but it took Nathanael Herreshoff to point that out, put it into practice, and change the way boatbuilders built their boats.

While most of the attention given to *Gloriana* at the time was focused on the obviously considerable overhang of her bow and stern, the real difference was below the waterline. The Seawanhaka Rule, under which *Gloriana* was designed, can best be explained as a "length-and-sail-area" rule, under which a boat was classified by waterline length and time allowances were made for the waterline length and the square root of the sail area. The result was the building of boats with large hulls on short, measured waterlines. The large sail area would "stand up" with the help of the boat's beam, draft, and ballast, as these measurements were "free," or not taken into consideration when calculating time allowances. The entirety of *Gloriana*'s ballast was external, placing it as low as possible in the boat and giving it a longer lever arm to resist heeling under the press of canvas. With a relatively narrow beam of 13 feet (giving a beam-to-length ratio of 5.46), the boat was almost entirely dependent on ballast rather than the hullform for stability, and the slender shape reduced friction.

The skills Nat learned in designing lightweight hulls for the steamboat contracts were put to good use with *Gloriana*. He reduced the wetted area of the keel by cutting away the forefoot, further reducing friction from the water. William Burgess designed most of the boats in the 46-foot class (Scotland's William Fife also designed a few), many of which featured very traditional-looking hollow clipper bows, but Nat removed the forefoot from nearly the entire length of the keel forward of the rudder post.

Some boats in the class had overall lengths less than *Gloriana*'s, notably *Harpoon* and *Mineola*, both Burgess designs, giving *Gloriana* more wetted length when heeled (and thus more speed). Her cutaway forefoot reduced the wetted area and the resultant friction, but perhaps more important was that Nat designed *Gloriana*'s lines to be roughly the same above and below the waterline. This kept the shape of the waterline roughly the same regardless of the angle of heel, reducing the amount of weather helm induced as the boat heeled. Increasing the rudder angle to counteract weather helm is tantamount to putting on the brakes; all other things being equal, the boat with a more neutral helm will go faster.

As well, with the ends of *Gloriana* drawn more full than those of the boats against which she was to compete, when she did heel, her center of buoyancy moved to leeward a greater distance than possible with the narrower designs, thus adding to stability even as the boat heeled. Thus designed to sail at considerable angle of heel, the boat took advantage of the gradual increase in waterline as her hull went over. A contemporary article in the *New York Herald* noted that the boat did

indeed measure 46 feet on the waterline when at an even keel, but that "when fairly close-hauled she measures about 65 feet on her actual waterline."

Gloriana's sails were products of the Herreshoff yard, as were a number of unique and lightweight items of deck and rigging hardware. In this respect, HMC was different from and superior to any of the other yards, all of which had to depend on the same stock parts available to everyone.

Gloriana's racing debut took place during the June 1891 Regatta of the New York Yacht Club (NYYC). Racing just outside New York harbor on the Sandy Hook Lightship course on a day described in NYYC records as "cold and wet—seas heavy and lumpy" with a strong northeaster blowing, only 11 yachts competed that day, four of which were 46-footers. Morgan's new boat, with either him or Nat Herreshoff at the helm (depending on who is telling the story), won her first race. Morgan did not participate on *Gloriana* during the port-to-port races during the NYYC's Annual Cruise that year; he was aboard one of his other boats, the 113-foot schooner *Constellation*, which won four of the five port-to-port races. The 46-foot class did compete, though, and given what followed, Morgan must have been pleased by the opportunity.

After the June Regatta victory, *Gloriana* went on to win her next seven races, with the only close call coming during the Goelet Cup races of August 7, when Charlie Barr, skippering the Burgess-designed 46-footer *Oweena*, maneuvered to a better start and, for a time, outsailed Morgan, who was sailing in company with Nat Herreshoff. After the win, Morgan withdrew *Gloriana* from racing for the remainder of the season to allow other boats chances at first-place finishes.

Morgan put up the boat for the winter, and with the coming of the 1892 season there were fears among members of the NYYC that *Gloriana* had effectively killed the 46-foot class before it had a chance to develop. That wasn't the case, of course—not as long as there were sailors who knew the way to Bristol, Rhode Island. Archibald Rogers, who had been racing his 70-foot *Bedouin* in 1891 commissioned Nat to design a boat that would beat *Gloriana*. The result was another milestone in yacht design. *Wasp*, design number 414, measuring 72 feet overall with the requisite 46-foot waterline, had a slightly bigger beam of 14 feet and just 2

inches more draft, at 10 feet, 8 inches, but the real news was the fin keel with a fully developed lead bulb keel. The ballasted keel allowed even more of the keel area to be cut away, and *Wasp*'s forefoot shows the shape of a true fin keel, albeit not as pronounced as it would be on later fin-keeled boats.

When Morgan learned of *Wasp*, he sold *Gloriana* after racing her for only a single season. But it was a season that forever changed how racing boats were designed and built. The success of the new 46-footer also did much to change the direction of Herreshoff Manufacturing Company and how clients and patrons perceived it. It was *Gloriana* that earned Nat the sobriquet "The Wizard of Bristol." The stunning racing success and distinctive lines of *Gloriana* produced a new look in boats, and spoon bows began to appear on boats designed on both sides of the Atlantic.

Rogers hired Charlie Barr to steer *Wasp*, while Barr's older half-brother, John, was aboard *Gloriana*, which Dr. W. Barton Hopkins had purchased. During the 1892 season, the two Herreshoff 46-footers faced off against each other several times, but in the end, Charlie and *Wasp* had the better record by a small margin. It seemed Morgan's instincts for boats were as finely tuned as his instincts for buying and selling stocks.

While the fight for 46-foot supremacy was taking place, Nat continued to design boats that turned heads with their ingenuity and originality. Early in October 1891, the

yard launched another boat for Nat's personal use. *Dilemma*, design number 412, was a fin-keeled boat that, while not the very first such boat, certainly attracted attention as though it was. The ballasted fin keel was invented in 1881 by an ex–Civil War colonel and amateur boat designer named Israel Garrard of Frontenac, Minnesota, who first fitted a 3-foot length of iron beam with a 1,200-pound cylinder of lead at the bottom onto the hull of a 22-foot sandbagger. Although Nat himself said he had not invented the ballasted fin keel, the popular sentiment was, and still is, that he did. It is fair, however, to say that he worked out the design details necessary to successfully apply the principle and that *Dilemma* was, in all likelihood, the first full-size yacht to be so equipped.

Dilemma, design number 412, was commissioned the same day as *Gloriana*, February 27, 1891, and predates the same design feature on *Wasp*, which was contracted on September 2, 1891. *Wasp*'s contracted price was $14,250 (about $281,000 today), coincidentally the same price contracted for *Gloriana*. While the yard's construction notes mention *Dilemma*'s new keel, stating succinctly that it had a "keel blade steel, lengthened 28 inches," no such mention was made for *Wasp*.

A conventionally rigged sloop with jib and main, *Dilemma* measured 25 feet on the waterline with a beam of 7 feet, 4 inches, and drew 5 feet, 9 inches. She had a very successful racing career, especially after being sold to a new owner, but was wrecked a few years later in Long Island Sound as she was entering the harbor. She was subsequently rebuilt, with an entire side reconstructed using lines taken from the remaining side, and is now on exhibit at The Mariner's Museum in Newport News, Virginia.

Wasp was built specifically to beat *Gloriana*, which she did. In the 1894 race season, *Wasp* won 10 of 14 races, putting to rest any critics who had attempted to ascribe to luck the success that *Gloriana* had experienced.

Just two weeks after *Wasp* was contracted, *Wenonah*, design number 415, another bulbed fin keeler, was begun to the order of Henry Allan, for the price of $1,935, just over $38,000 today. *Wenonah* was very similar to *Dilemma*, measuring 37 feet, 6 inches LOA, and 25 feet LWL, with a beam of 7 feet and a draft of 6 feet. With a balanced rudder, long overhangs, and the ballast down low in a bulb that appeared almost heart-shaped in cross section, she and especially *Dilemma* were the smaller precursors to *Drusilla*, the last boat contracted at the HMC yard in 1891 and listed as design number 417. E. D. Morgan wanted a boat for sporty afternoons on the water, and, considering that *Drusilla* was 50 feet on deck with a 35-foot waterline, conceivably he thought he might have a pocket cruiser, as well.

In January 1892, Morgan was elected commodore of the NYYC, and although there were some mentions that a 35-foot boat was not big enough for the commodore of the prestigious club, in fact Morgan's flagship that year was the 226-foot G. L. Watson–designed steam yacht *May*. *Drusilla*'s hullform had more beam and less depth than other bulbed fin-keel boats, to give her form stability before the ballasted fin keel began to take effect, typically at 15 to 20 degrees of heel. This was done in the interests of comfort, to allow the boat to sail more nearly upright. With some stability from the hullform, Nat reduced the ballast, but the result was that *Drusilla* sailed on her ear anyway. She was taken out of the water and a new, heavier bulb was attached. The modification provided the necessary stability, but the additional weight submerged the intended waterline.

One reason for overhangs is that when a boat is heeled, the effective waterline is lengthened, thus increasing the hull speed without increasing the wetted area. But when the boat is down on her marks, the increase in waterline is more than offset by the considerable increase in wetted area. *Drusilla*, now stiff enough to stand up to her sail, performed acceptably to windward, but in the words of Nat was "hopelessly beaten off the wind."

Vigilant, 128-feet LOA, was ordered by a NYYC syndicate. She would be Herreshoff's first America's Cup defender, winning three straight races against challenger *Valkyrie II*. *Mariners Museum*

Nat had his crew of shipwrights begin another *Coquina* for his own use, making the design slightly longer and narrower, with 3 inches less draft. But a sailor from Minneapolis, Minnesota, named W. P. Hollis decided he wanted it, and the yard records show that design number 419, listed as "Coquina 2nd," had the names "N. G. Herreshoff" and "W. P. Hollis" written above it in the "Built For" column. Hollis paid just $350 for the boat, or about $7,000 today.

Some of Nat's sailing vessels began to attract overseas clients, as well. The diminutive fin keeler *Wee Win*, design number 425, was built for Eloise Cochrane, of Bideford, England, and measured just over 16 feet on the waterline with 4 feet, 6 inches beam and a draft of 3 feet. *Wee Win* was so successful that fin-keel boats were effectively barred from competition. The outlawing of fin-keeled boats was effectively done by the way the boat was measured for its rating. Local yacht clubs

Nat Herreshoff talking with a friend, or an employee, on the dock at Herreshoff Manufacturing Co. The boy sitting on the bollard is Nat's son. *Mariners Museum*

employed a rating rule that specified "girth difference," that is, the difference in the measurement from rail to rail along the hull (using "skin girth," or the actual surface distance) and the so-called "chain girth," the distance measured by a tight string or chain from the rail and over any concavities caused by slack bilges or, more specifically, a fin keel. The difference in these two measurements was then added to the boat's other measurements. A boat with a round hull would produce identical numbers; one with a fin keel would produce two very different numbers and a ratings penalty.

As with most attempts to outlaw a design advance, the "girth difference" rule soon failed, because the speed advantage derived from the evolution of the fin keel to the bulbed fin keel, with its much-reduced wetted area and low ballast, soon made the rule obsolete. Bulbed fin keels were here to stay, and the designs and boats of Nat Herreshoff, who produced at least half of all such designs in the waning years of the nineteenth century, led the way.

It was the contract for the 84-foot LWL cutter *Navahoe*, though, in September 1892, that set the course for HMC's reputation as *the* yard for big, fast sailboats. *Navahoe* was commissioned by Royal Phelps Carroll—the same Carroll whose pending marriage had caused him to exit ruefully from the contract that was to become Morgan's *Gloriana*. In *Navahoe*, design number 429, Nat designed a boat that drew so much water, 13 feet with the board up, that the area around the pier had to be dredged to provide enough water after her launch from the South Shop. The boat was designed with a centerboard, but, extrapolating from the yard's records, may have begun as a keelboat, as there is a crossed-out check under the category listing it as having a fixed keel.

The big cutter, 123 feet on deck, was the first HMC boat built of steel, and Carroll lost no time in taking her out on the racing circuit. To skipper the boat, he engaged the services of Charlie Barr, for whom the experience of sailing such a large boat was fairly new. *Navahoe's* sea trials in early May 1893 marked the first time either Barr or Nat sailed such a big boat, and, in the words of her designer, "we had much to learn."

Carroll had his eye on setting a transatlantic record, and, with his wife aboard, he and Barr set out from Newport with the spinnaker flying, determined to make a fast passage to England, where he intended to match his boat against England's best. As the *Navahoe* passed south of Nantucket, she entered a fog bank, and, sailing by dead reckoning, ran smack into the Nantucket New South Shoals light ship.

Barr was the subject of some disparaging comments at the time for this apparent display of bad seamanship (Nat's son, L. Francis Herreshoff, sarcastically states in the biography of his father that Barr's navigation was "remarkably good—for you might say he was less than a ship's width off the course"), but none of the critics apparently were aware that the light ship, the 100-foot overall *LV 54*, had been placed on duty November 13 of the previous year, and that the position of the light ship had been moved 10 miles southwest of where the previous light ship, *LV 1*, had been anchored since 1856. It is thus very likely that Barr, unaware of this move, fully expected to miss the light ship by at least 10 miles and had set a course giving him enough berth to allow for any tidal set.

The collision sprung the mast of *Navahoe* and Barr had to turn around and make for Boston for repairs. The mast was replaced, but the yard there had neither the skills nor the materials that HMC did, and *Navahoe* ended up with a mast that was technically inferior and physically heavier. Weight aloft is critical for a sailboat, as it contributes to the amount of heel produced by the wind. The farther a boat heels, the more the effect of weight aloft is felt, and with *Navahoe*, which was acknowledged by her designer as lacking stability because of her shallow draft, the effect was even worse.

Nat was aware of the boat's problems, and after her sea trials he put her back in dry dock. The lead ballast was removed from inside the hull and placed on the keel, with enough additional lead added to increase her draft by 12 inches. Undeterred by the mishap with the light ship, the Carrolls and Barr set off again for England, making a fast, but not record-setting, passage. *Navahoe* raced against the British royal yacht *Britannia* for the Brenton Reef Cup, which James Gordon Bennett, publisher of the *New York Herald Tribune*, had donated in 1872. The Cup was first awarded for what is still considered the first ocean race, starting off Newport and won by the yacht *Genesta*. It had been held by the British since 1885. *Navahoe*, with her heavy rig and insufficient stability, was not at her best going to windward, and the course, from the Needles at the west end of

the Isle of Wight to Cherbourg, France, and back, was a 60-mile reach each way in strong easterlies. The two boats were evenly matched, never more than a hundred yards apart for the entire race, and the finish was after sunset, with the boats finishing within seconds of each other.

The finish-line judges awarded the prize to *Britannia*, skippered by the Prince of Wales, but Carroll protested, stating that the finish line was not straight and that *Navahoe* had actually crossed first. The matter was given over to a race committee, and after much deliberation, they reversed their decision and awarded the Cup to *Navahoe*.

The two boats met again a few days later to contest the Cape May Challenge Cup, which turned into a drifting match over the same Needles–Cherbourg–Needles course. *Britannia* easily won this race, keeping the Cape May Cup, which had been brought to England in 1885, also by the big cutter *Genesta*, and then held by the British plank-on-edge cutters *Irex* and *Wendur*.

Despite *Britannia* winning the Cape May Cup, it was the beginning of the end for British boats, many of which were built narrow and deep, typically with a beam-to-length ratio of 6:1. The shallow, beamier American boats, as exemplified by those being designed by Nat

A Buzzards Bay 15 set up for a dry-land portrait. Nat Herreshoff's second one-design class followed the successful Newport 30s.
Herreshoff Museum

Herreshoff, were winning most races. By 1887, helped by a change in rating rules, there were no more plank-on-edge boats being built in England; by then, the style had virtually disappeared in the United States, as well.

Navahoe's racing record in England was not the stuff of legend, and winning back the Brenton Reef Cup was the highlight of her European racing tour. In 13 starts, she only won twice and then returned to America, where she won the Goelet Cup in 1894 and 1897. These victories must have been very sweet for Carroll. In the 1894 contest, run in a 12-knot southwesterly, he raced against both *Wasp* and *Gloriana;* in 1897, he raced against another Herreshoff boat, the ex–America's Cup defender *Vigilant*, winning the last Goelet Cup race ever. The sponsor of the Cup, NYYC member Ogden Goelet, died in 1897, and as he had renewed the Cup's sponsorship annually and made no provision for its continuance in his will, its 15-year history died with him.

The Herreshoff yard in the 1880s and 1890s was awash with boat orders, many of them for smaller boats. But two one-design classes—the Newport 30 in 1895 and the New York 70 in 1899—created at the behest of the NYYC and its members, added measurably to

the reputation of HMC as the only place to go if winning yacht races was your goal. A third one-design—the Buzzards Bay 15—fitting neatly in between the two big NYYC classes, was organized in 1898 for sailors who preferred the lively sailing afforded by a smaller boat. These latter boats, only 15 feet on the waterline, were so small as to be undetectable by the NYYC.

The Newport 30, although not an official New York Yacht Club class because of their small size, may as well have been—13 of the 14 boats produced for the class were owned by NYYC members. The two men who owned the fourteenth boat were later made members of the club. The fin-keeled Newport Thirties, 42 feet overall as designed by Nat in 1895, were exactly 30 feet on the waterline, 8 feet, 4 inches beam, and drew 7 feet, 4 inches. Class rules specified they be no longer than 43 feet, with LWL between 29 and 30 feet. The beam was open. Sail area had to be between 956 and 1,000 square feet. These were strictly racing boats, with large cockpits and no accommodations. They carried a crew of four, and the rules allowed as many as three of them to be professionals. In a spirit of magnanimity, one woman was allowed on board as well, possibly the result of the NYYC's decision in 1894 to allow women as members, providing, of course, that they owned a suitable yacht. In fact, the class is notable for the fact that many of them were raced with women aboard. The woman who catalyzed this change was Lucy Carnegie, widow of Thomas Carnegie, brother of Andrew. In preparation for this membership bid, she commissioned the 119-foot screw schooner *Dungeness* in January 1894 (but not from the Herreshoff yard).

The Newport Thirties were not quite a Herreshoff monopoly—two were built by other yards and designed by NYYC members. The contracted price for a Newport 30 was $2,850, roughly $60,700 today, and the idea of making a fleet of identical boats was still a fairly new one, although its attractions were obvious; even then no one could completely agree on how to measure a boat to calculate true handicaps.

For the story of the Newport Thirties to be told properly requires backtracking a few years to the design, in November 1893, of the biggest fin keelers made at the Herreshoff yard, the so-called "20-raters," the sister ships *Niagara* and *Isolde*, design numbers 449 and 450, respectively. Both boats were built under the Seawanhaka Rule, which favored long overhangs, with the attendant advantage of a rule-beating, shorter LWL, and a shallow hull, made easier with the adoption of the fin keel. *Niagara* went to England after sea trials and *Isolde* to Germany. In the case of *Niagara*, her racing success was such that the boat truly became the one to beat.

The two cutters measured 65 feet overall on a 45-foot waterline, with beams of 12 feet and a draft of 10 feet, 8 inches. The price was $12,500, some $260,000 today.

They were racing boats, pure and simple, with a flush deck, virtually no accommodations because of the shallow hull (less than 5 feet of headroom), and a cloud of sail above with a boom extending well past the transom. The two boats were famed for both their speed and the quality of their double-planked construction, and they certainly owed much of their speed to new crosscut sails, invented by Nat that year. Because he could find no sail loft to make sails with the bolts of cloth running perpendicular to the leach, he had them built at the HMC yard, adding to the "one-stop shopping" policy for which the Herreshoffs were known.

The first set of crosscut sails went on *Houri*, design number 442, a 21-foot LWL fixed-keel sloop, contracted on April 1, 1894. The second set went on Nat's 28-foot LWL sloop *Alerion*, design number 446, in June of the same year, another example of the designer's personal boat being used to test his ideas. (The name Alerion is a term from heraldry, referring to an eagle displayed with wings spread.)

The owner of *Niagara*, Howard Gould, was also a part-owner of *Vigilant*, the successful Herreshoff-designed America's Cup defender in 1893, for her English racing campaign in 1894.

Nat took the lines from *Niagara*, reduced them in size to fit the one-design standards for the Newport 30, and came up with a small, nimble day racer that was immensely popular, given that there were only 14 of them built. The class raced regularly on Narragansett Bay, with several races every week during the summer sailing season. The comparatively narrow keel and the balanced rudder made for a boat that would turn in its own length.

Of the 12 Newport Thirties the yard turned out, all were ordered between November 15, 1895, and April 24, 1896, with seven of them ordered on November 30 alone. They were all built with identical molds, upside down in the Herreshoff manner. It is a tribute to the skills of the shipwrights and the organizational talents of J. B. Herreshoff

Nat Herreshoff's 28-foot *Alerion* sailed extensively in Bermuda waters for a decade, before returning to the United States. This beautifully built *Alerion* sails off the coast of Massachusetts. *Cory Silken*

that they were all built in the course of one winter, while the yard was also busy turning out four other smaller sailboats and an 85-foot steam yacht.

When the NYYC, in the course of revising the race rules, decided on a new class in 1899, they called it Class I, which fit nicely between Classes H and J. The boats became known as the Newport Seventies, the biggest one-design fleet ever designed, and while they were spectacular to look at and exciting to race, the price, $32,593.75 (one has to wonder where the 75 cents came from), equivalent to over $700,000 today, made them the exclusive playthings of the very rich. Only four were ever built, two of which were owned by Vanderbilts.

Once the class was established, though, the five owners (one, *Yankee*, was jointly owned) went immediately to Bristol and on October 11, 1899, ordered their boats, each with their own design number, 529 and 532 through 534.

With an overall length of 106 feet, overhanging a waterline of 70 feet, the Seventies pushed the structural limits of conventionally built wooden boats. They were truly immense, carrying 6,000 square feet of sail with some 40 tons of lead in the keel, a 14-foot draft and nearly 20 feet of beam. Two of the owners of the Seventies had been racing Newport Thirties, and they took the hard-driving racing

habits formed with the smaller boats with them, setting the tone for the Seventies.

Under the duress of hard racing, the boats began to develop problems. The long overhangs put tremendous stresses on the hull. After a windy race during their first season, the summer of 1900, all four boats in the fleet opened their seams to the extent that they barely made it back to port. When racing was finished that year, the fleet was laid up and two lengths of 7/8-inch steel cable were run from stem to stern, passing under the mast step, in hopes of reducing the sagging problems.

The Herreshoff yard came under some criticism for the boats as their problems became more well known, but eventually even the NYYC was convinced that the root of the problem lay with the Seawanhaka Rule, rather than in any innate flaw in design or construction. Nat had known for some time that a rule which virtually required that a boat be built with massive overhangs would create its own set of problems. After much discussion, he proposed to the NYYC what became known as the Universal Rule, which factored in displacement as well as length and sail area.

While it was the big boats that made the headlines and a good part of the Herreshoff reputation, the closing years of the nineteenth century saw the beginning of what was one of HMC's most popular and well-loved boats: the Buzzards Bay 15, also known as the 503 after the design number of the first one, built in 1898. Chronologically it was the second one-design, after the Newport 30, but with a price of $666.66 (again that calculation to the very penny), equal to just over $14,000 today, it was vastly more popular and eventually nearly a hundred of them were built. They were all 24 feet, 6 inches overall, with a waterline of 15 feet and a beam of 6 feet, 9 inches. The long keel, with 1,000 pounds of lead ballast, drew 2 feet, 4 inches, but had a centerboard incorporated for better windward performance.

There were several variations on the theme: some had fixed keels drawing as much as 4 feet, 2 inches, and one had an extended bowsprit and a larger rig to enable her to compete in the Long Island Sound 21-foot class. For the most part, though, they were strict one-design boats. Sixteen were built in the months before the yard was occupied with the Seventies, and by the time the last one of the nineteenth century was built, in October 1899, the price had only gone up to $700. The

Physalia is a classic version of the original *Alerion* of the early 1900s. *Cory Silken*

class had something of a last hurrah in the form of the Watch Hill 15s, built in 1922 using the 503's molds but with a Bermudan rig instead of the gaff main of the original Buzzards Bay 15s. Another variation was the Newport 15, identical but with the keel 6 inches deeper.

The boats were also known as the E-class, and among their features were a watertight compartment fore and aft. But perhaps just as important is that the boats were made light, with speed rather than longevity the defining element of the scantlings specifications. The boats required careful maintenance, and became known for being easily sprung when pushed too hard, a temptation hard to resist on a boat that was a joy to sail.

The Buzzards Bay 15, though, was an unqualified success, and its reasonable price, plus the advantages offered by a one-design class, ensured that the yard seemingly always had one in the shop at some stage of construction. They were beloved by their owners, and, even today, more than 100 years after the first one hit the water of Narragansett Bay, you still see them, sometimes out on their own, sometimes gathered in a fleet of lovingly maintained wooden boats built by the Herreshoff yard.

For the latter years of the nineteenth century, the HMC yard was busy with boats, most of them for private owners, but sandwiched in between the yachts were the boats that made the design genius of Nathanael Herreshoff truly international in recognition and influence. Those boats were built for the various syndicates that put up their money to defend challenges to the America's Cup—boats so special they deserve their own chapter.

Nat's Cup Boats of the Nineteenth Century

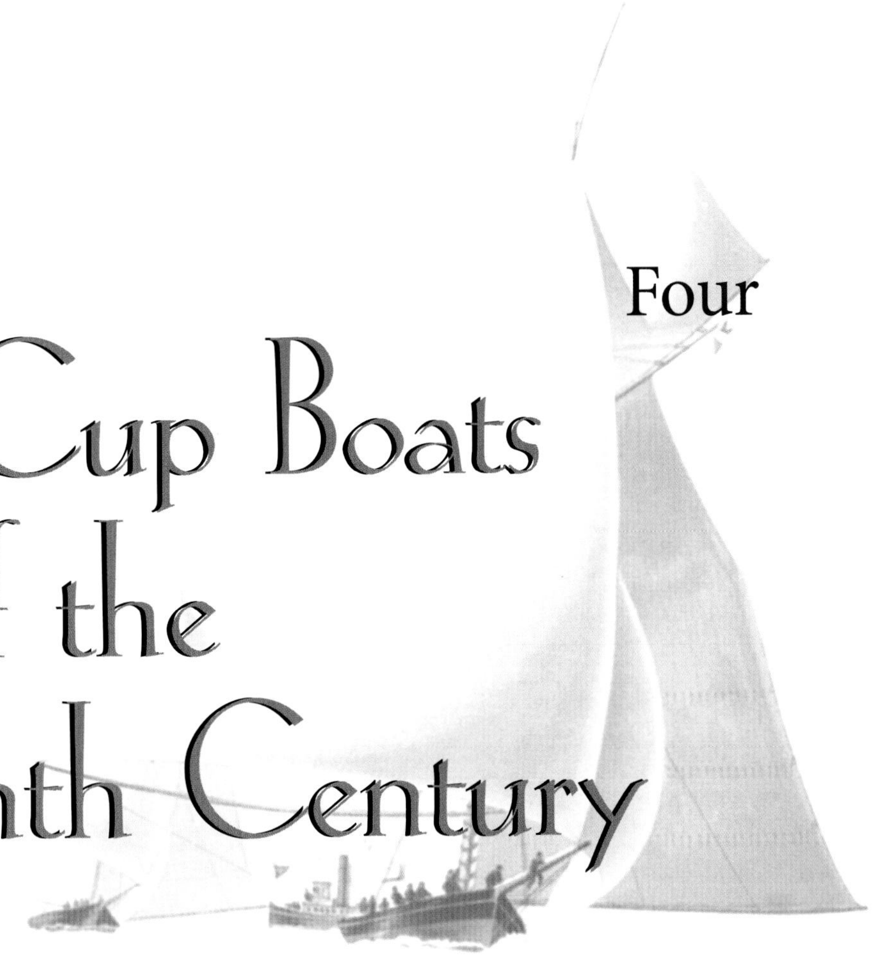

The America's Cup contest, from its beginning in 1851 with the race around the Isle of Wight and the celebrated victory of the American sloop whose name became attached to the trophy, to the present day, is the world's preeminent sailing trophy. The sport's greatest names, from designers to sailors to the syndicates who band together to fund the campaigns, have been associated with the trophy, a rather gaudy silver urn with the nickname "the hundred-guinea cup," allegedly its cost of manufacture. That works out to an 1851 value of around $9,000; not an insignificant sum, but one that pales in comparison to the cost of mounting a Cup campaign.

Opposite page:

Defender, seen here in dry dock, carried the greater part of her 177,000 pounds of ballast in the bottom of her keel. *Herreshoff Museum*

A Cup race begins when a yacht club formally challenges the holder of the Cup. The race is actually a series of races, the exact type of which is established by the defending club. In fact, nearly every aspect of the race is determined by the holder of the Cup, giving the defender very much of a "home court advantage."

The Cup contests prior to 1893 have been well documented, as, indeed, have all the Cup races, and thus only a short background of that year's races is necessary to understand the contributions made by Nathanael Herreshoff and the Herreshoff Manufacturing Company. The races are held to no schedule, occurring when a challenge is made to the club holding the Cup and that challenge is accepted. In those years and many thereafter, the New York Yacht Club held the Cup, which was on permanent display in a glass case at their New York City headquarters.

In 1893, a challenge was mounted by Windham-Thomas Wyndham-Quin, fourth Earl of Dunraven and Mount-Earl, of Dunraven Castle, Brigend, Glamorgan, Wales and of Adare Manor, Adare County, Limerick,

An early painting of the start of the America's Cup race of 1881 pits the American yacht
Mischief against the Canadian *Atalanta. Mischief* retained the cup for the NYYC.
Mariners Museum

Ireland (to give him his full name), a wealthy Irish sportsman whose racing yachts had enjoyed a regular series of victories in England and Europe. The last Cup race prior to 1893 had been in 1887, and Lord Dunraven, through the Royal Yacht Squadron of Cowes on the Isle of Wight, felt he had a yacht, the G. L. Watson–designed cutter *Valkyrie II*, that would bring the Cup home to England. The challenge was made in the autumn of 1892, with the race to be held the following year.

Events leading up to the challenge were fractious indeed. On the evening of the final race between *Thistle* and *Volunteer* in 1887, after the NYYC boat had retained the Cup, the Royal Clyde Yacht Club, sponsor of *Thistle*, delivered a preliminary challenge to the NYYC at its Madison Avenue clubhouse. The NYYC nearly ignored the challenge, but did give it enough attention to write a new Deed of Gift for the Cup, coming up with rules giving the defender such a clear advantage that it seemed for a time there would not be any further challenges.

The new deed was roundly denounced by foreign yacht clubs. Finally, in April 1889, Lord Dunraven sent a challenge, sponsored by the Royal Yacht Squadron (RYS), with his first *Valkyrie* as the challenger boat. The NYYC accepted this challenge, perhaps pleased the storm over the new deed had apparently settled. However, in a lengthy series of letters, the RYS stated they felt the new Deed of Gift so favored not just the defender but the NYYC itself, that should they lose the Cup and become a challenger, it would be an unfair contest. The members of the New York club, naturally, felt the RYS was being churlish and were not correctly interpreting the rules. The RYS withdrew its challenge in June 1889.

It took until September 1892 for Dunraven, again with the sponsorship of the Royal Yacht Squadron, to send another challenge. In the intervening years Dunraven had stayed in touch with the NYYC through the services of an Englishman, Joseph R. Busk. Busk was a NYYC member who had successfully defended the Cup with his 70-foot sloop *Mischief* against the Canadian challenger *Atalanta* in 1881. In December 1892, the New York club accepted the challenge. Among the race terms Dunraven requested was that it would be a best-of-five contest and the deadline for the first race would be October 5, 1893, giving the NYYC just ten months to fund, design, and build a boat.

Dunraven already had a boat. In his letter he announced that his boat of challenge was to be *Valkyrie II*, a composite-built keel boat with the long overhanging bows and cutaway forefoot by then made familiar in Herreshoff boats. It was such a successful design component that it had become virtually standard for racing boats. Dunraven's boat was sheathed in copper, with the sheathing extending above the waterline at the ends to keep the hull sleek when heeled over. *Valkyrie II*'s designer, the Scotsman G. L. Watson, was no stranger to Cup boats; his cutter *Thistle* lost to the Edward Burgess–designed centerboard sloop *Volunteer* in 1887, and he would go on to design more Cup boats. *Valkyrie II* was very similar to the British royal yacht *Britannia*, also a Watson design.

The agreement between the NYYC and the RYS stated that the boats were to measure 85 feet on the waterline, a number that Dunraven was presumably happy with, despite his *Valkyrie II* measuring just over 86 feet LWL. (That seemingly became the target number; the eventual defender measured similarly.) Four American syndicates were formed almost immediately to commission boats to vie for the honor of defending the Cup. Burgess had been the man to see for America's Cup boats, having designed successful defenders in 1885, 1886, and 1887, but his death in 1891 at the age of 43 of typhoid cut short a very promising career.

Two of the four syndicates went to Nat for their boats; the other two syndicates each went to a Boston yard for their boats. Archibald Rogers, a familiar face at the Bristol boatyard, headed one of those syndicates. He had commissioned *Wasp* (see Chapter 3) the previous year, and the syndicate noted that the Herreshoff yard had, in construction at that time, the steel-hulled, 84-foot waterline *Navahoe* (also discussed in Chapter 3).

Rogers specified that their vessel, to be named *Colonia*, should not draw more than 14 feet, the depth of water at his home at Hyde Park on the Hudson River. Although Nat was not comfortable with this draft for a boat that was 126 feet overall with a beam of 24 feet, he drew the boat as asked. Interestingly, the yard records state the boat's draft as 15 feet, despite evidence that the ways at Bristol could not handle a boat with more draft than 14 feet. In an essay by Nat on the subject, he refers to *Colonia* as only drawing 14 feet and writes that was "plainly not enough for an 85-foot waterline."

Colonia, design number 435, was commissioned December 13, 1892, indicating that the syndicate placed the order as soon as possible after the challenge was accepted. *Navahoe* was occupying the South Shop at that time, and the yard was busy with a variety of smaller craft, as well. *Navahoe*'s work schedule was put in high gear; she was launched in February 1893 and moored in a dredged hole to accommodate her 14 (or 15) feet of draft.

The contracted price for *Colonia* was $45,000, nearly $900,000 today, truly a significant sum. The members of Rogers' syndicate reads like a who's who of the Gilded Age, men whose net worth made such a purchase an affordable luxury: W. K. Vanderbilt, Frederick W. Vanderbilt, J. Pierpont Morgan, F. Augustus Schermerhorn (the director of Consolidated Gas Company of New York), and John E. Brooks (of Brooks Brothers). A professional skipper, Henry C. "Hank" Haff of Islip, New York, was hired to steer the boat, a sailor with impeccable credentials, having successfully steered *Volunteer* to victory over *Thistle* to successfully defend the 1887 Cup.

Colonia's hollow spars were built at the C&R Poillon boatyard, in Brooklyn, New York, of Oregon pine, staved in the manner of a barrel but two layers thick. Each stave was 1 1/2 inches thick, and there were circular bulkheads at regular intervals to which the staves were attached. The spacing of the bulkheads was determined by the presumed stress at particular places, and it was all held together with

Members of the Royal Yacht Squadron, December 6, 1894. From left to right: Kaiser Wilhelm, Earl of Dunraven, Rear Admiral the Honourable Victor Montague, The Prince of Wales, The Marquis of Ormonde, and The Earl of Lonsdale. *The Royal Yacht Squadron*

Vigilant, the second of two Herreshoff boats ordered by American syndicates to defend the Cup in 1893, was the eventual winner over the challenger *Valkyrie II. Mariners Museum*

Astor Carey, and Dr. W. Barton Hopkins. The contracted price for the boat was $55,000, an even more magnificent sum, equivalent to more than $1 million today. The Herreshoff yard was about to have a very good year.

The Morgan syndicate named their boat *Vigilant*. She measured 86 feet, 2 inches on the waterline, 124 feet overall, and with a beam of 26 feet, 3 inches was fully 2 feet wider than *Colonia*. *Vigilant* was a centerboard cutter, with a centerboard weighing nearly 4 tons and a hull made of polished Tobin bronze, a copper/zinc/tin alloy noted for its resistance to seawater corrosion. The alloy was a relatively recent formulation, invented just a few years prior by a U.S. Navy lieutenant named John Tobin.

Because of the bronze hull, *Vigilant* proved to have a much more sleek hull than did *Colonia*, whose steel hull had problems with scaling and was never as fair as the polished bronze of *Vigilant*. With her 16-foot-6-inch board up, she drew 13 feet, 6 inches, and so was just able to float in the water of the launching ways at the South Shop. With the board down, she drew 24 feet.

Nat wasn't about to have *Vigilant* lack stiffness, and with a sail area of 11,272 square feet, she would plainly need some weight down low. The centerboard was 3 1/2 inches thick, made of 7/32-inch Tobin bronze plates and the inside filled with molten lead to a weight of 7,750 pounds. The top of the centerboard was covered with broken coke and made smooth at the top with a layer of cement. The board was raised and lowered with a geared chain winch designed for that purpose by Yale & Towne Company of Stamford, Connecticut, later to become known for their locks. The centerboard was a source of regular difficulties. If the chain was paid out too quickly, when lowered the board would jam because it was hinged on a cast bronze hook set in a plate riveted to the keel.

Vigilant had a 16-inch-deep lead keel, a development begun with *Navahoe*, which originally had her lead ballast placed in the bottom of the bilge. When *Navahoe* was found to be tender, the lead was taken out, recast into plates, and bolted to the keel plate. *Vigilant's* original design called for the lead to be similarly placed, but the sea trials for *Navahoe* took place while *Vigilant* was still on the ways, and the change in *Vigilant's* ballast location was made rather early in the building process. Her final displacement was a staggering 192,000 pounds, or 96 tons

screws, glue, and wraps of wire cable overlapping the bulkheads.

There was some uneasiness among members of the NYYC regarding *Colonia's* ability to keep the Cup in its case at the club's headquarters (even though at that time two other syndicates were building boats), so Edwin D. Morgan, who became the NYYC's commodore that same year, put together a fourth syndicate after *Colonia* was in construction, commissioning Herreshoff design number 437 on February 9, 1893.

Morgan was joined by a group of men no less impressive than those in the Rogers syndicate. They included August Belmont (grandson of Commodore Matthew Perry, banker, railroad magnate, and developer of the Triborough Subway and Cape Cod Canal), Oliver H. P. Belmont (developer of Belmont Park racetrack, who would marry W. K. Vanderbilt's ex-wife Alva two years later), Cornelius Vanderbilt, Charles R. Flint (New York City banker, organizer of U.S. Rubber Company, founder of IBM), Chester W. Chapin (Boston & Albany Railroad, Western Railroad, Chapin Steamship, and the New York subway system), George C. Clark, Henry

Vigilant was built of steel frames with steel topsides, and although the 70-man crew lived aboard, her interior was spare in the extreme. G. L. Watson, possibly in the course of checking out the competition, remarked that the furnishings "amounted to little more than a coat of paint."

The number of crew became a point of contention, with critics pointing out that 70 men amounted to movable ballast. Valkyrie II had a crew of 40, so the windward weight of Vigilant, figuring an average crew weight of 160 pounds per man, was 11,200 pounds. The boats were measured without crew, however, so with her full complement of crew aboard, Vigilant gained something on the order of one foot of unmeasured waterline, calculating her hull immersion factor of 8,076 pounds per inch. This was noted by, among others, a writer in the November 25, 1893, issue of Forest & Stream magazine:

Assuming the right of Vigilant, in default of any express prohibition, to avail herself of this kind and amount of ballast, there is still the nice question of ethics; whether such a course is to be considered fair and sportsmanlike. This much may safely be said, that had it been Valkyrie instead of Vigilant that thus took advantage of a plain defect in the rules, there would have been a greater clamor than was raised over the alleged over-length of Thistle in 1887; and further, that it is one of those tricks which can be played just once.

The non-dimensional numbers for Vigilant are telling, indeed, especially compared to those of the challenger, Valkyrie II. The sail area-to-displacement ratios—Vigilant's being 54.19 and Valkyrie's being 48.43—are, by today's standards for anything outside of racing multihulls or extreme lightweight monohull ocean racers, virtually off the chart. With Vigilant's slight advantage, one would expect her to be better in light airs.

In a comparison of displacement-to-length ratios, an indication of how easily driven the hull will be, one would expect Valkyrie to have the advantage, with a displacement-to-length ratio of 130 carrying a slight edge over Vigilant's 134. The two were close in displacement, with Vigilant weighing in at

Vigilant and Valkyrie II in a thrash to windward during their Cup races of October 1893.

Vigilant against *Jubilee*, another American yacht built to defend the Cup in 1893.

Mariners Museum

192,000 pounds and *Valkyrie* at 190,600 pounds. *Vigilant*, however, was the more slender of the two, with her beam-to-length ratio of 3.28 comparing favorably to *Valkyrie*'s 3.89; *Valkyrie*'s much slimmer hull, at 22 feet, 4 inches beam, was why the pounds per inch immersion numbers are so different. *Vigilant* calculated to 8,076 pounds per inch and *Valkyrie* to 6,916, but even with this lower figure, the challenger carried 30 fewer crew and so had less weight on the windward rail and less weight to settle the boat down on the marks and produce unmeasured waterline.

Two other American boats were built for the 1893 challenge, and although their performance soon proved inferior to the Herreshoff boats, they are worthy of note. The sponsoring syndicates were both from Boston. *Jubilee* was a steel sloop of novel design, by John B. Paine, the 20-something son of General Charles Jackson Paine, who, as a NYYC member, had been involved in three earlier Cup contests. As the manager of several railroads, including the Atchison, Topeka & Santa Fe and the Chicago, Burlington & Quincy, the elder Paine was qualified, in that most important respect, to be a member of the syndicate that built the Burgess-designed *Puritan* in 1885 before taking on the costs of

two more Burgess Cup boats: *Mayflower* in 1886 (a campaign for which he was also the manager) and *Volunteer* in 1887.

The younger Paine drew *Jubilee*, a combination fin-keel centerboarder with a smaller centerboard forward of the main keel/centerboard. The bills were paid by his father, who referred to *Jubilee* as "my son John's boat." The boat was built by the George Lawley & Son yard of Boston, a very reputable operation, and skippered by John Barr, but the design just didn't work. The boat carried so much lee helm as to be nearly unmanageable, and even when she could hold a course the rigging was weak. John Paine nevertheless remained an amateur yacht designer, and his younger brother, Frank C. Paine, would design the J-class *Yankee* some 40 years after John forayed into yacht design.

The other non-Herreshoff American boat built for the 1893 America's Cup was *Pilgrim*, designed by Stewart and Binney. The steel centerboarder was such a failure as a sailing vessel that she was converted to steam the next year.

When *Vigilant* was finally built, Morgan bowed out of active management and turned the campaign over to C. Oliver Iselin, who became the project manager. Iselin's grandfather had become suitably wealthy in the importing business, and in 1877 was elected a member of the NYYC. The younger Iselin crewed aboard *Volunteer* in 1887 and his position as *Vigilant* project manager was the first of many Cup campaigns for which he was the manager. As usual, the syndicate hired a professional skipper, selecting William Hansen, who had previously skippered a privately owned schooner named *Sachem* but had no notable experience as a racing skipper.

The trial races began as soon as all the defenders were in the water, with *Vigilant* launched June 14, a month after *Colonia*. It wasn't a lengthy selection process, but there were a few rogue waves to deal with. After the first trial race, with Nat and Iselin aboard, among others, Iselin felt that *Vigilant's* relatively poor performance could be improved with a different skipper and asked Nat to take the wheel. From the second trial race to the final victory, Nat drove the boat he designed.

The two Boston boats were eliminated from contention very quickly. The first elimination race for the hopeful defenders took place on September 7, and over three days of racing, with a lay day in between each, *Vigilant* tied with *Colonia* the first day and won easily on the succeeding days. *Colonia's* inconsistent performance made the choice of *Vigilant* to defend the America's Cup an easy one. (While the final stages of selecting the defender were taking place, Dunraven was in the process of bringing his boat across the Atlantic. It was a lengthy voyage, and *Valkyrie* arrived on September 22 after a very stormy passage of 29 days.)

Because Cup boats of those days were not built to class specifications as rigid as those today, they were handicapped. *Valkyrie*, carrying "only" 10,042 square feet of sail—1,230 square feet less than her opponent—and with nearly identical waterlines, was thus given one minute, 48 seconds.

The first race started on schedule, October 5, off Sandy Hook, but it was a light air day. The race, like nearly all sailboat races, had a maximum time, in this case 6 hours. *Valkyrie* was far ahead, having caught some light airs, but when it became apparent that she could not finish within the time limit, the race was called. Two days later, a 30-mile windward-leeward race began in a moderate northwesterly that fairly soon backed to a southerly favoring *Vigilant's* tactics and position. What had begun as a windward beat turned into a reach and the

C. Oliver Iselin, syndicate manager for four consecutive NYYC America's Cup defenders. *Herreshoff Museum*

C. OLIVER ISELIN

return was a run, with *Vigilant* winning by 5 minutes, 48 seconds, corrected time. Nat's helming was flawless—in fact, it was his skippering of *Vigilant* in this race that gave him his most well-known sobriquet from that point onward of "Cap'n Nat."

The races of those days were public spectacles, with a fleet of boats surrounding the race course and inevitably getting in the way. The accumulated wash from the spectators following the lead boat interfered with the trailing boat, another of the complaints regularly made by the challengers.

The next race, on October 9, featured a moderately strong sou'wester over a 30-mile triangular course, and *Vigilant* led for the entire race, with Cap'n Nat covering *Valkyrie* to her

Vigilant's crew preparing the mainsail before the 1893 series of Cup races. *Library of Congress*

windward at every tack. The last leg was in a hatful of wind and *Vigilant* sprung her bowsprit in the 30 knots that were blowing near the finish, but nevertheless won by 10 minutes, 35 seconds on corrected time.

With *Vigilant* leading 2 to 0 in the best-of-five series, the October 11 race was canceled for lack of wind, putting what could be the final race off until Friday the 13th. Superstitions, however, were set aside, and the race took place in spite of a forecast that called for a gale to work its way up the coast. The race was a 15-mile beat to windward and back, with winds of 15 knots at the start. Before the boats crossed the start line, *Valkyrie* broke the sheave that handled the throat halyard, and things were postponed for more than an hour while the crew effected repairs.

After the boats finally set off, *Vigilant's* centerboard gremlins went to work. The man in charge had let it fall too quickly and the chain jammed against the board, preventing it from fully dropping. Once they had forced it down halfway with a jury-rigged tackle, they found it could not be forced back up for the downwind leg. Despite all this, *Valkyrie*

rounded the windward mark 2 minutes ahead of *Vigilant*.

Vigilant had made the beat with a full reef in the main and carrying a working topsail, whereas *Valkyrie* put in half a reef, giving her more sail area while working to windward. On the run back to the finish line these differences in sail handling became apparent. The English were in the habit of doing flying sets with their spinnakers, launching the huge sail by hauling it up as quickly as possible while the unset portion billowed around the deck. The American method was to set the sail with stops, easily broken ties of light line that bundled the spinnaker into a sausage shape. The sail was then broken out either by cutting the stops or allowing the force of the wind to break them once the sail began to fill.

Valkyrie's spinnaker caught on a deck fitting, and a small tear beginning in the foot soon spread until the sail was destroyed, with ribbons of torn fabric fluttering in the growing wind, hitting 25 knots as the race went on. Dunraven's crew took in the spinnaker and set the linen light-weather spinnaker in its place, but this was fouled on the bitts (post-like fittings

The Earl of Dunraven's *Valkyrie III*, a George L. Watson design, running before the wind. *Mariners Museum*

made to secure dock lines) before fouling the jib topsail itself. Doubtlessly frustrated with the whole process, Dunraven's skipper, William Cranfield, set what the English called a bowsprit spinnaker, known in the United States as a balloon jib topsail. Even this attempt was plagued as the halyard jammed and a man was sent aloft to clear it. They made no attempt to shake out their half-reef on the main.

On the American boat, things were going more smoothly. *Vigilant* set her stopped spinnaker, with the sheet and tack slack, and then set her balloon jib topsail. With the wind rising as the boats ran before it, Cap'n Nat sent four men aloft. One, attached to a halyard, was pulled along the main boom with the outhaul, cutting the reef pennants as he went; a second was at the mast trucks, ensuring all lines ran fair; another was at the topmast trucks, with similar duties; and the fourth was at the end of the gaff. They reset the working topsail, lashing the head to the topmast and the clew to the end of the gaff boom. The now-free sheet and halyard were then sent down and bent onto the second club topsail, which was hauled aloft and set to windward of the working topsail. The reef on the main was shaken out and the mainsheet was run out. With nearly every sail in her inventory flying, *Vigilant* took off, clawing back the two minutes with every wave.

Three miles from the finish, with *Vigilant's* board half down and *Valkyrie* struggling with her sails, the two boats were even, with Cap'n Nat working every puff of the ever-increasing wind until he crossed the line ahead of *Valkyrie* to win with a corrected time lead of just 40 seconds. So impressed were the members of the NYYC that Lord Dunraven was voted an honorary member. The Cup, however, remained in its case in the club's headquarters, then at 60 Madison Avenue, and the stage was set for the next challenge, in 1895.

Vigilant was bought that winter by NYYC members George J. and Howard Gould, sons of Jay Gould, apparently to lay to rest the complaint that, while challengers had to be capable of making an ocean passage, the defenders were free to build a delicate racing boat that could not cross seas. The revised Deed of Gift said, in effect, "All racing boats must arrive at the race on their own bottoms," a ruling that was fair enough in the eyes of the NYYC.

The Goulds commissioned Cap'n Nat to strengthen their new boat, and he supervised the addition of diagonal braces of steel angle iron along the inside of the hull connected to T-braces running fore and aft under the deck. He also added bulwarks and lifelines and set a smaller rig. Confident in the boat's seagoing strength, the crew set out from Brooklyn for Scotland on June 1, 1894. Leander Jeffries skippered the passage, with

Haff engaged as the racing skipper. Cap'n Nat was invited to come along, and he followed *Vigilant* across aboard the Gould's steam yacht, *Atalanta*, along with Haff. They arrived in Gourock, Scotland, on June 16, and the Gould brothers wasted no time in lining up some races—after a quick visit to a boatyard in Glasgow to remove all the bracing.

Vigilant's first race in Scotland set the tone for all subsequent races in British waters, and it was eventually enough to convince Cap'n Nat that his energy would be better spent back in Bristol. How he came to that conclusion involved club politics, bad luck, technical problems with the boat, and a suspicion of ethics not quite at their Sunday best. The night before the first race, on July 4, the regatta committee of the Mudhook Yacht Club, the race's sponsoring club, notified *Vigilant's* crew that all yachts in the next day's race on Holy Loch had to be helmed by an amateur, a category for which Haff was not qualified. Cap'n Nat was persuaded to take the helm. The racing fleet facing *Vigilant* consisted of a refitted *Valkyrie II*, a new *Britannia*, *Satanita*, and *Iverna*, all massive cutters. On race day

there was ample wind and a spectator fleet crowding the course. Just before the start, the 98-foot LWL *Satanita*, the largest boat in the fleet, charged up to the start line before the gun. A rain squall had obscured the course, and Cap'n Nat shortened sail down to main and jib, with *Britannia* just to windward.

As the squall cleared, *Satanita's* crew saw a small boat with four men aboard in her path and luffed up to miss them, but then, way lost, the big boat was unable to bear away afterward and collided with *Valkyrie*, cutting 6 feet into the deck and opening her up below the waterline. The two yachts became entangled and swung in a deadly circle until *Valkyrie* fouled on a spectator's steam yacht. This freed her from *Satanita* and, breaking free of the steam yacht, *Valkyrie* sank in 14 fathoms of water. One man was killed, Dunraven and his guests were taken off, and, amazingly, *Vigilant* and *Britannia* continued the race.

Britannia won, almost entirely by virtue of Cap'n Nat taking advice from the local pilot they took aboard who sent him on a course that avoided a favorable, and well-known, localized afternoon breeze originating off a point of land. The disgusted Cap'n Nat wrote in his notes, "After this I did no more racing yachts for others."

Vigilant raced *Britannia* a total of 17 times that summer, winning five races. She had regular problems with the centerboard, finally losing it entirely after running aground. Upon her return to the States she was sold, in 1896, to NYYC member Percy Chubb, who altered the rig to a yawl in 1901. Chubb sold her in 1903 to F. Lothrop Ames of the Eastern Yacht Club, who in turn sold her a year later to NYYC member Stephen Peabody. That same year, 1904, Peabody sold her to William E. Iselin, who used her as a cruising boat until 1909. In 1910 the gallant *Vigilant* was broken up and many of her fittings used in the Cary Smith–designed schooner *Enchantress*. Along the way, she served as a trial horse for the 1895 Cup trials (as did *Jubilee*).

Cap'n Nat, for his part, returned to Bristol before the English racing season was half over. Business at the yard was booming, and there was nothing he seemed to prefer to designing and building boats—not even racing them.

And what of *Colonia*, seemingly doomed to failure before she was launched? After the Cup trials she was rerigged as a schooner, had her name changed to *Corona*, and in her new guise had a successful racing career, winning the Goelet Cup in 1892 and 1896, and the Astor Cup in 1900 and 1902. She served as the flagship of the NYYC from 1900 to 1902 and finished out her days as a tender for the W. Starling Burgess–designed J-class *Enterprise*.

Dunraven, who was still eager to compete, sent another challenge to the NYYC in the autumn of 1894, beginning with a lengthy letter to J. V. S. Oddie, the club's secretary. In his letter, Dunraven addressed the problems with the massive numbers of crew carried on *Vigilant* and the effect that weight had on waterline, stating that "yachts should be measured with all the weights on board, dead or alive, which they intend to carry during a race." He also requested the venue be changed from Sandy Hook to Marblehead, to reduce the problems presented by the spectator fleet. More importantly, he wanted the challenger to be able to state the challenge with several boats and select the best one, just as the defenders did in their trials races. After much deliberation, the NYYC agreed to measure the boats in racing weight, but would not move the venue. They did agree to allow a

second challenger, a concession that must have pleased and surprised Dunraven.

With all of the letter writing, the challenge process stretched out until January 1895 when the NYYC finally accepted the challenge, sponsored again by the Royal Yacht Squadron. Dunraven would race *Valkyrie III*, another Watson boat measuring 89 feet LWL. The NYYC would be represented by a syndicate, again managed by Iselin, and including W. K. Vanderbilt and E. D. Morgan.

Cap'n Nat had not been idling away at the boatyard awaiting the next commission, however. The lessons learned from the Cup contest of 1893 and races abroad were many, and the yard was still busy with the usual run of clients. Among the problems *Vigilant* had in England, along with a busy racing schedule, was that her sails had stretched so badly that they lost their shape and had to be re-cut. Nat had problems with English sail makers, but then he

Valkyrie III and *Defender* just before the foul. The large steamship to starboard is almost certainly the one that interfered with the 1895 race. *Mariners Museum*

Valkyrie III at speed with all sails set. *Mariners Museum*

had problems with American sail makers, too. The bolts of cloth from which the sails were made ran vertically—that is, parallel with the leach—because cloth made as it was back then stretched less if the strain was applied across the warp (the length of the bolt of cloth). Additionally, there was greater wind resistance with the seams running vertically. As far back as 1850 there had been attempts to make crosscut sails, but problems with the cloth made them impractical.

Cap'n Nat set to the task of first designing sailcloth, and then the crosscut sail. He commissioned canvas duck, woven to his specifications, from the Lawrence Manufacturing Company, a textile firm in Lowell, Massachusetts, that made everything from sailcloth to underwear. When he received the cloth, the first set of crosscut sails went on *Houri*, design number 442, a 21-foot sloop begun on April 1,

1894, and the second set went on one of his personal boats, the 28-foot *Alerion*, design number 446, begun June 17.

Of the many inventions that Nathanael Herreshoff came up with, his crosscut sails probably have seen the most application. Boats too small or too traditional to use sail tracks still have crosscut sails, even if their fiberglass hulls weren't built upside down or with bronze screws.

The syndicate for the defender came to the HMC yard to sign the contract on January 23, 1895, making her the first boat of the year. The contracted price was $75,000, a staggering sum in those days before income taxes, equivalent to nearly $1.6 million today. Cap'n Nat had not been happy with the restrictions placed on the design of *Colonia* by her syndicate, and, as this next boat would be even bigger to match *Valkyrie III*'s 89-foot waterline, he couldn't make it a centerboard boat. The

On board *Defender* under sail; the crew at action stations. *Library of Congress*

design had to be a keelboat. He had the bottom dredged around the launching ways and the docks, thus freeing him in the boat's draft. The name was decided after a contest among schoolchildren; a six-year-old girl won with the name *Defender*. While there was criticism that the name was rather too generic, it stuck.

Defender was built with one goal: to keep the Cup. She was extremely light and was the first American yacht built using aluminum. The frames were made of bulb angle steel, very much like standard angle iron but with the angles terminating with a thickened section. Bulb angle iron was used for steamship construction, but those frames were too big for a sailboat that would have every component weighed. Cap'n Nat drew the cross-sectional shape, designed the rollers, had them made, and contracted the work to a foundry.

The steel-framed hull was plated with Tobin bronze from the waterline down, and with aluminum above the waterline. The deck beams were also aluminum, as were the diagonal straps that braced the hull. The deck was wood, the last Cup boat Herreshoff so built. After that, the decks were metal, covered with either cork or unpainted canvas.

Aluminum was still relatively new as boatbuilding material; it had only been 30 years since an affordable method was invented to extract it from its ore. The British navy had built a few torpedo boats of aluminum, but it was still so rare that the shipwrights in the Herreshoff yard took the punchings from the hull's panels home with them to show their children. It was a light, strong metal that didn't rust—it seemed perfect for boatbuilding. Aluminum is, however, very reactive when placed in contact with nearly any other metal in the presence of an electrolytic fluid. Salt water is an extremely good electrolyte, and when *Defender* was finally launched, with her gleaming bronze hull, aluminum topsides, and steel frames, she must have fizzed like an Alka-Seltzer tablet.

Defender was built under conditions of near-military secrecy. With no restriction on draft, Cap'n Nat gave her 19 feet of it, but with a narrower, more easily driven beam of 23 feet. *Valkyrie III*'s designer, again Watson, had apparently decided that *Vigilant*'s bigger beam let her better stand up to a head of sail, and so he drew *Valkyrie III* with a beam of just over 26 feet and a draft of 20 feet. *Valkyrie III*

Defender's crew in 1895.

Library of Congress

was cutter-rigged, compared to *Defender*'s sloop rig, and the challenger had a slight edge in sail area, carrying 13,028 square feet. *Defender* carried 12,602 square feet, but they were Nat's significantly more efficient new crosscut sails.

Comparing the two boats' non-dimensional numbers is, again, very illustrative. While Watson's latest *Valkyrie III* resembled the Herreshoff boat that had defeated his boat in 1893, with greater beam and more draft, Herreshoff's boat was deeper and narrower than anything he had done before, with a ballast ratio of 55 percent. The displacement-to-length for both boats was the same, with *Valkyrie III*'s slight extra length compensated for by a slight addition in displacement. *Defender* was much slimmer, with a beam-to-length of 3.85, compared to the challenger's 3.4. But the real difference is apparent when comparing sail area to displacement: *Defender* measured 58.96, *Valkyrie III* 60.35. The pounds-per-inch immersion shows *Valkyrie III* having the greater capacity, with 8,297 compared to *Defender*'s 7,273, a number that reflects the greater beam of the Watson boat.

The first race, begun on September 7, was laid out as a windward–leeward race, but as the light 6-knot breeze swung to the east, the race became a beat and a reach. With all the con-

cern about ballast, the boats were carefully measured before the race, and a committee led by Archibald Rogers and fellow NYYC member A. Cass Canfield marked the load waterline of *Defender*. *Valkyrie III* left the measuring area at Erie Basin before she could be marked.

At the start, it appeared that *Valkyrie III* was the faster boat, but *Defender* was able to point higher, and at every tack she pulled ahead. By the time *Valkyrie III* rounded the weather mark, she was three minutes and 28 seconds behind, and for the entire last leg *Defender* continued to pull ahead, beating *Valkyrie III* by eight minutes, 49 seconds, corrected time.

Dunraven entered a protest against *Defender*, alleging that extra ballast had been taken aboard, but measurements taken after the protest, with G. L. Watson in his bathing suit and marking his boat and Nat Herreshoff doing the same, but from the security of a rowboat, revealed both boats to be exactly on their marks. The false accusation was based on the fact that the *Defender* crew had taken some of the lead pigs off the boat and cut them up to fit them more compactly. They were returned to the boat, but chicanery was suspected, nonetheless. The charge was made quietly, with no public notice, and disposed of just as quietly, after measurement proved the accusation to be non-substantive.

At start of the second race on September 10, *Valkyrie III's* 105-foot boom fouled the starboard topmast shroud of *Defender* in the course of a turn on *Defender's* weather side. Haff and Iselin broke out the protest flag and continued the race, with their protest acknowledged by a gunshot from the committee boat.

Defender's crew tried to effect a repair while continuing on the triangular course, but had to douse the jib topsail and rounded the first mark nearly three minutes behind. They made up time on the final two legs, losing by just 47 seconds on corrected time.

Dunraven said the collision was the result of *Defender* luffing unnecessarily, but the protest committee disagreed, citing photographic evidence proving Iselin's claim that *Defender* had held her course and *Valkyrie III* had luffed into *his* boat. Dunraven also claimed that the spectator fleet had made navigation difficult, and indeed the collision sequence had its beginning when the two boats crossed on opposite sides of a large steamer sitting behind the start line.

The actions of the steamboat were noted by, among others, the reporter for the *New York Times*, who wrote that the poor seamanship evidenced by the steamboat skipper was "one of the most unpardonable interferences ever seen in American yachting waters."

The protest committee awarded the race to *Defender.* Iselin offered to re-sail the race, but Dunraven refused, and instead insisted to the special committee sent to talk with him that they declare the next race void if there was spectator crowding. They said they had no such authority and so the third race took place on September 12, with the spectator fleet now kept well back. *Defender* came to the line with all sails set for the light northwesterly, and *Valkyrie III* appeared with just the main and jib, carrying no topsail. *Defender* crossed the start line first, followed nearly two minutes later by *Valkyrie III*, who broke out her NYYC burgee, took a line from her tug, and proceeded back to her dock. The unannounced retirement shocked everyone, and when Iselin came to the finish line, he asked the committee boat if he should finish the race. They replied in the affirmative, and *Defender* won the third race unopposed.

Dunraven returned to England and made further and public charges that *Defender* had surreptitiously added ballast. The Royal Yacht

Squadron maintained that it was a personal squabble between Dunraven and the NYYC, leaving Dunraven to retain the services of a lawyer and show up for two days of a five-day hearing at the NYYC. The NYYC was sufficiently upset over the accusation that they published a 556-page report on the matter, clearing Iselin from any wrongdoing. Dunraven refused to apologize, and the NYYC then proceeded to expel him, an action that was followed later by Dunraven's letter of resignation.

And what of *Defender*? Retired Cup victors are often used as trial horses for subsequent Cup boats, but the mix of metals in *Defender* doomed her from the moment she first sat in salt water. She was built to win, and only had to last long enough for that. Despite being nearly completely rebuilt in 1899 for the Cup trials, she was broken up in 1901.

There was yet one more Cup race, in 1899, to close out the nineteenth century. It was the first of the Sir Thomas Lipton's series of five *Shamrocks*, and it is a story best told consecutively.

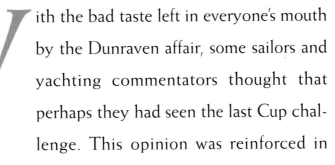

Five

Lipton and the Twentieth Century

W ith the bad taste left in everyone's mouth by the Dunraven affair, some sailors and yachting commentators thought that perhaps they had seen the last Cup challenge. This opinion was reinforced in September 1895 when Charles Day Rose, through his club, the Royal Victoria Yacht Club of Ryde, England, made a challenge. The New York Yacht Club accepted the challenge and set the match for 1896. As the Dunraven furor grew, Rose decided to withdraw his challenge, fearing it would be seen as a tacit "expression of opinion on the results of the last race," as he stated in his withdrawal telegram.

Opposite page:

Columbia under a full spread of canvas during the Cup races of October 1899.

Library of Congress

In the latter part of 1895, after Rose's withdrawal, another English sailor had asked the Royal London Yacht Club to forward a challenge. The club refused to forward the challenge, stating that the Deed of Gift as the NYYC had written it was "inimical to the sport of yacht races."

It wasn't until August 1898 that things began to look up for the NYYC when they received a challenge from a man who had, literally, never put his hands on the helm of a sailing vessel. Sir Thomas Lipton owned a very finely turned-out 252-foot LOA steam yacht, *Erin*, and he also owned a yachting cap. Of much greater importance was that he owned the Lipton Tea Company and had a bank balance suitable to ballast a sailing yacht of any size necessary to challenge for the America's Cup.

Lipton challenged through the Royal Ulster Yacht Club of Belfast, Ireland. Lipton's name had been put to the far more prestigious Royal Yacht Squadron for membership, sponsored

Sir Thomas Lipton made five unsuccessful challenges for the America's Cup.

Library of Congress

by his friend the Prince of Wales, but the blue-bloods of that club felt that Lipton, who had been knighted in 1898 but lacked any pretentious family background, was not their cup of tea. Lipton had left school at the age of ten and summed up his business philosophy by saying that the secret of his success was to "open a new shop every week." He was far more than a purveyor of tea; his grocery stores supplied all the United Kingdom and Ireland, and he had led a life that, in its self-made success, was more of an American style of story than it was British.

Indeed, Lipton was an admirer of America and Americans. The British furor over the Cup, accompanied by a considerable amount of anti-American sentiment, bothered him greatly, and one of the reasons he decided to make a Cup challenge was to show his countrymen that Americans weren't the bounders and mountebanks that some members of the British press and yachting society felt. He had spent his latter teenage years working in the United States, and had good memories of his time there. His business interests had by then gone considerably beyond merely selling tea; he owned meatpacking plants in Chicago and Omaha, Nebraska, and was as noted for his philanthropy as he was for his wealth.

The members of the NYYC knew very little of this at the time; they didn't even know if Lipton could sail. But they welcomed his challenge, seeing it as the salvation of the Cup. Lipton's lack of sailing skills was noted in the press, with the British magazine *The Field* stating "He does not appear to have had any extended experience in yacht racing." The article went on to venture the opinion that the NYYC would view the challenge as "absurd, and the club would naturally decline to entertain it."

The NYYC did no such thing, and instead accepted the challenge immediately. The rules required the challenger to name and describe his vessel. Lipton had wanted a boat that would be, in its entirety, a product of Irish craftsmanship, but the yard he contacted in Belfast, Harlan and Wolff, felt they weren't capable of making a yacht, despite their experience with having built all of the liners for the White Star Line, and so declined the honor. Instead they recommended Thornycrofts, at Chiswick and Millwall, near London on the Thames River. They had considerable experience with metal hulls by virtue of naval contracts, having built a series of torpedo boats

noted for their speed. An Irish designer was similarly elusive, and Lipton engaged William Fife Jr. of Fairlie, Scotland. Lipton presented to the NYYC the boat *Shamrock*, 128 feet LOA with overhangs of 39 feet. The big cutter had a beam of 25 feet and drew 20 feet, 3 inches.

The lessons of *Defender*'s mix of metals had not yet been fully learned, and Fife specified bottom plating of manganese bronze with topsides of aluminum. The notice of a challenge had little of this information, however, stating only the boat's name, the load waterline of 89 feet, 6 inches, and that she was cutter rigged.

With the opposition now announced, and Cap'n Nat's recent victories, there was only one place to go for a defending boat. The syndicate was headed by J. Pierpont Morgan, commodore of the NYYC, with C. Oliver Iselin as the project manager, both veterans of previous Cup challenges. On September 28, 1898, the contract for the cutter *Columbia* was entered in the Herreshoff ledger as design number 499. She had a contracted price of $90,000, nearly $2 million today, but the purchase price was just the beginning, as any boat owner will confess. By the end of that first season after her launch in June 1899, the syndicate had spent $250,000, about $5.3 million today. It was obvious that this was a race the NYYC didn't intend to lose.

Morgan took a very personal interest in the project, and contemporary reports noted that all the expenses were borne by him, thus showing that Morgan was "well and plenteously equipped with patriotism and sportsmanlike spirit," according to Capt. A. J. Kenealy, a well-published nautical writer of that period. That he was also "well and plenteously equipped" with cash certainly helped.

In Bristol, design and construction began with a major project to enlarge the launching area at HMC. The ways were lengthened, to 300 feet, and the bottom was dredged to accommodate boats with a 20-foot draft. The biggest improvement apart from the increase in size was the installation of a marine railway to ease the launching process. While HMC had been making boats at a steady rate, they had been mostly smaller boats. Before *Columbia*, there had only been four sailing vessels bigger than 50 feet LWL, and it was the beginning of a new era for Cap'n Nat, J. B., and the yard.

In the next 17 years the yard would build some of the greatest, and biggest, steel yachts ever designed, and the financial health of the company would increasingly rely on the big commissions rather than the steady production of smaller yachts and daysailers. It was also around the turn of the century that Cap'n Nat's naval contracts ended. It began with a general disaffection he felt for working with such a large bureaucracy. The Navy would second-guess his decisions, and he preferred working with millionaires. They not only paid on time,

they ordered the boats and then sailed them away. Not so with the Navy.

The turning point came in 1894, with the delivery of design number 185, a sister ship to design number 184, both 175-foot, 6-inch overall torpedo boats with twin screws and two four-cylinder, triple-expansion engines. The naval contractors told Cap'n Nat that, in their opinion, the piston guides were made of the wrong sort of steel. Against Nat's better judgment the guides were replaced. When, during sea trials the guides heated up so badly as to make the vessel's safe return a matter of speculation, Cap'n Nat made up his mind that he was not going to deal with military contracts again.

Nat Herreshoff never worked well with people who tried to tell him what to do. When those who gave him instructions were proved to be wrong, as was the case with his racing in Scotland, the design oversight he suffered with *Colonia*, and now, with the Navy's inspectors, he saw it as proof that he knew best. And who was to argue? His boats won races, his designs were emulated worldwide to the extent that he often found himself racing against what amounted to a copy of his last design, and HMC was selling boats as fast as the skilled workforce could produce them.

With the shift to big sailing vessels as the company's financial mainstay, the size of the boats that rolled out of the HMC yard steadily grew. The dredged area around the launching area could now accommodate vessels with greater draft, and with bigger boats came greater profits. From the turn of the twentieth century to 1915, Cap'n Nat designed, in addition to the Cup boats *Columbia*, *Constitution*, *Reliance*, and *Resolute* (totaling 470 feet overall), seven large steel-hulled schooners, with a total waterline length of 645 feet, and another six totaling 404 feet of waterline of private yachts simply built for the pleasure of the owners. The money was rolling in, and almost certainly Nat didn't miss the Navy. J. B. was another matter entirely: driven by the profit motive, he saw the contracts as a surefire moneymaker, and as he didn't have to deal with engineers second-guessing his decisions, it is likely he missed that additional source of revenue.

With the building of *Columbia* proceeding, Morgan's syndicate needed a trial horse, and for this they selected *Defender*, which had to be rebuilt practically from the keel up, an expense that Morgan also bore.

Columbia's hull was made of Tobin bronze, but instead of the aluminum topsides used on *Defender*, Cap'n Nat opted for nickel steel. Cast brass was used for the stem and sternpost, as well as the keel, made in three sections. In order to cast the keel, the refit of *Defender* had to be completed; with this done by mid-January 1899, the casting was completed 10 days later. There were two masts made for *Columbia*, one of Oregon pine and another of hollow steel, and a separate hollow steel mast was made for *Defender*, which was fitted at the conclusion of her refit. The choice of a steel mast was made for the reduction in weight that it offered, and *Defender* had to add nearly one ton of ballast to get her back down to her designed waterline. *Columbia*'s steel mast was set aside, and the pine version was stepped upon her launching.

The launching of *Columbia*, June 10, 1899, was not without its share of drama. Drawing 19 feet, the dredged launching ways proved insufficient, and she stuck fast in the mud for nine hours until the crest of the tide lifted her clear. A crowd said to number in the thousands attended the launching, and as night fell, the brilliant, white glare of calcium lights illuminated the entire scene.

Photographers also attended the nighttime launching. They each held trays of highly flammable magnesium powder over their head to provide the light for a photograph. One of the photographers misjudged the amount of powder, and when the powder went off, inadvertently it seems, the roar and flash was such that it lifted people nearby off their feet and a five-year-old boy was thrown from his perch on the launching tramway into a coal pit, where he bled to death in a matter of minutes. Other spectators were cut and bruised, and J. B., likewise there for the celebration, was the victim of a pickpocket who relieved him of $200.

Sea trials began two weeks later, with a crew selected from among the sailors of Deer Isle, Maine, with Capt. Charlie Barr as skipper. After half a season's trials with the Oregon pine mast, with the benefits of a steel mast having been proven on *Defender*, *Columbia* returned to the HMC yard on August 24 to have the hollow steel mast fitted. Intrinsic to this mast, the first such used on a Cup defender, was a telescoping wood topmast, and the lighter weight of the steel mast, compared to the pine version, materially improved *Columbia's* righting moment. The mast was not met with universal approval, even before it was used. After the mast was stepped, J. B. went over to it and tapped it with his walking stick, the one engraved with the measuring notches. He expressed an opinion to his brother that the mast wouldn't work, that it would "buckle at the first strain."

His thoughts notwithstanding, the mast was rigged. The reduction in weight was nearly 2,000 pounds, just as with *Defender*, and the crew set out, with Cap'n Nat, C. Oliver Iselin and his wife aboard. In a race against *Defender*, off Newport, the first race with the new mast, J. B.'s skepticism became prescience. A spreader broke and the mast collapsed. By a stroke of random good fortune, no one was injured, despite Iselin and Cap'n Nat standing near the spot where the mast hit the deck. The race was before the NYYC's annual cruise, where she was to be the star of that event, and after she was towed back to the facilities in Bristol, the pine mast was refitted, and *Columbia* was just one day late in joining the cruise.

The match races against *Defender* continued, and while *Columbia* was regularly the winner, her margins of victory were initially not of the magnitude expected. It took the crew most of that 1899 season to polish their racing skills, and when the repaired steel mast was restepped, their newly found abilities were augmented by the improved ability of the boat to stand up to the wind by the reduction in weight aloft.

Shamrock, too, used steel masts and booms, but they were a source of constant trouble to

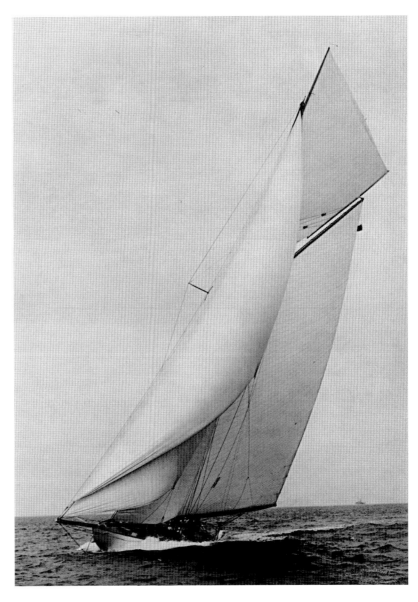

the challenger's crew, even though, as was the case with *Columbia's* masts, they were internally braced. The mast of *Shamrock* had regular problems with bending, not to the point of collapse, but it made setting the sails a problem, and *Shamrock's* crew went through six sets of sails in an effort to find ones that were right.

The races began on October 3, with the expectation that the later date would provide a more certain chance for wind. The first race saw winds so light the boats could not finish in the prescribed time, and the same thing happened at two-day intervals, on October 5 and 7, although most observers agreed that *Shamrock* was the superior boat in light airs. Fog plagued the next races, sitting so densely on the course there wasn't even a start, despite attempts on October 10, 12, 13, and 14.

Finally, on October 16, the weather cooperated. Among the spectators was Guglielmo Marconi, inventor of the radio, the absolute

With her lee rail under, *Columbia* is up to speed and reveling in a good breeze. *Library of Congress* latest in the technical marvels of the age, who had been contracted by NYYC member James Gordon Bennett, publisher of the *New York Herald*, to send news of the race to Bennett's paper. The rival papers, with their carrier pigeons, would find themselves so far behind the *Herald* in getting out the news to a public that was hungry for results that it would trigger what amounted to an informational arms race with the American press. Marconi used a tall mast to send the news, supported by wire stays and looking very much like a sailboat's mast. It was from this race that the new triangular sails, replacing gaff sails in that era, became known as Marconi rigs.

At the helm of *Columbia* was Cap'n Nat, who occasionally turned it over to Barr. Some members of the press and crew objected to Barr's presence in any capacity; only "full-blooded Americans" were supposed to man the boat, and Barr, a naturalized citizen, didn't make that mark, or so they thought. With *Columbia's* first victory, the jingoistic hubbub abated.

The second race foretold the final results; *Shamrock's* topmast collapsed during the windward leg of the triangular course, she was towed to her berth, and *Columbia* crossed the finish line alone. The third race, after yet another cancellation due to lack of wind, was on October 20, a windward-leeward event, in accordance with the pre-race agreement stipulating alternating the two types of courses.

Captain Nat Herreshoff was either aboard or watching his America's Cup defenders from a tender close by. *Mariners Museum*

Shamrock had installed a new topmast and fitted additional ballast, resulting in a re-measurement. Sitting lower in the water, her handicap was adjusted and she went from *Columbia* owing her time to having a lower handicap. From the dead calm of the previous race, the weather had turned right around, with the wind blowing 20 knots from the north.

The start was somewhat unusual in that it was to leeward, with the wind blowing the boats across the start line. With Barr at the helm, *Columbia* crossed the start a minute behind *Shamrock*, possibly a tactical decision, desiring to blanket *Shamrock* with his spinnaker by following behind the challenger. He had trouble with the big sail in the high winds, and finally dropped it, setting a working topsail in its place, the same combination *Shamrock* used. He passed *Shamrock* just before the leeward mark, and the two boats rounded it nearly neck-and-neck. On the final, windward leg, *Columbia* was faster whether hard on the wind or with the sheets eased for speed, and crossed the finish line six minutes, 18 seconds actual time, and six minutes, 34 seconds on corrected time, thus keeping the Cup in its place at the NYYC headquarters.

Columbia wasn't the favored boat with the American touts, who were giving *Shamrock* the edge at odds of 6 to 5. Cap'n Nat had no such doubts; having been given a free hand in the design of *Columbia*, his faith in the boat never flagged, even after the collapse of the mast. In England, Lloyd's of London favored *Columbia* as well, with the oddsmakers favoring the defender 3 to 1.

The occasion of the victory marked another lifetime event for Cap'n Nat. Stepping below after the race, he joined Barr in the cabin and noticed he had a glass in his hand. When he found out that Barr was celebrating with a tot of whiskey, he said, "I think I'll have some." That was the first, and last, drink that passed the designer's lips.

With the race over, Cap'n Nat went aboard William Randolph Hearst's *Vamoose*, the 112-foot LOA steamboat designed by him in 1890. When he arrived in Bristol, just after sundown, a party was already underway. He, J. B., and the Herreshoff Manufacturing Company, were the heroes of the day in Bristol. At J. B.'s house on High Street, a joyous crowd had gathered, most of them HMC employees but with a sizable percentage of Bristol's citizenry as well.

J. B. finally gave in to the repeated requests from the crowd to deliver a speech, something he was neither prepared for nor comfortable doing. He rose admirably to the occasion. Beginning with a modest recap of his life, he thanked the people of Bristol for never losing faith in a blind man who wanted to build boats. He remembered the steady flow of orders for catboats, rowboats, and even rope, the rope he made himself at the ropewalk he had built. Their support made it possible for HMC to return the favor, he said, by becoming a major employer in the town, sharing in the prosperity he and his brother had found through their mutual endeavors.

J. B. was not, by nature, a speechmaker. Like his brother Nat he shrank from the limelight, wasn't a man to wade into a crowd, and while he was quite pleased that the name Herreshoff was known worldwide as the maker of fast, race-winning sailboats and equally fast, dependable steamboats, he would just as soon the attention remained on the company, not him. Or even on someone else. "So now," he said, "hurrah for Nat Herreshoff!" With that, he picked up his cane-cum-measuring stick and led the crowd to the DeWolf house, the small farm just outside of town where Nat's wife, Clara DeWolf, had been spending the summers. Cap'n Nat rarely visited there, preferring his aerie at Love Rocks where he worked in solitude. He was there for this occasion, as were many other members of the Herreshoff extended family.

Inside the house, the family members heard the noise outside, with the crowd shouting Nat's name in unison. His wife, Clara, urged him to the door, to just say a few words to his supporters and fans. The crowd shifted from calling out Nat's name to singing "*Columbia*, the gem of the ocean," and Nat, gathering courage by raising his oldest son, Algernon Sidney, to his shoulder, stepped onto the porch. The yard was illuminated by torches carried by the throng, and Cap'n Nat stood in the glare as though transfixed. He was literally speechless, but faced with a multitude of cheering supporters, he managed a smile and a wave of his hand.

Clara had seen to it that a barrel of cider had been laid in, expecting a crowd after she learned of the victory, and soon the barrel sat in the front of the house. By morning the barrel was empty but, when the bell rang at the HMC yard at 7 a.m., there were no absentees.

In New York City, Lipton was given honorary membership in the NYYC and was feted at a dinner. At both the dinner and a luncheon shortly after the race, aboard the *Erin*, Lipton showed the world a level of sportsmanship that had been lacking in some previous Cup contests, toasting the winning boat and her designers, stating that, "Mr. Herreshoff has shown himself to be the greatest designer of yachts in the world."

He had not resigned himself to being a graceful loser, however. Suffixed to his speeches was the statement, "I shall return." He might have added, "and soon," because his next challenge arrived at the NYYC in October 1900. His boat was to be the *Shamrock II*, 89 feet on the waterline and cutter-rigged. In the challenge, Lipton specified a series of race dates beginning in August 1901, perhaps hoping to avoid the doldrums and fog of previous autumnal races. The same method of alternating triangular and windward-leeward races was proposed and Lipton also asked that no racing would start after 1 p.m., and that the maximum time be shortened half an hour from the previous race's six-hour time limit. The NYYC agreed to both.

With the acceptance of the challenge, members of the NYYC had to begin the task of commissioning yet another race boat. There was no debate as to who would design it, but this time it wouldn't be J. Pierpont Morgan who would be funding the enterprise. A syndicate

Showing her graceful lines and with all sails pulling, *Columbia* speeds past a steam launch.
Mariners Museum

Reliance was the largest single-master ever built. She stood 189 feet 6 inches from her topmast sprit to the waterline. Her 28 feet of forward overhang can be clearly seen here. The black smoke drifting past is from a spectator steam yacht in the background. *Mariners Museum*

boat to use longitudinal framing, a method that is now virtually universally used in the building of large vessels, which provided great strength for the hull and helped the web frames maintain the shape. The frames also were well suited as attachment points for standing rigging and the keel, spreading that load over a wide area. Another significant advantage of the longitudinal framing was that the hull plating, made of Tobin bronze, could be directly attached to it, providing a smooth, seamless finish to the hull. The web frames were situated at every fourth angle frame, and the longitudinal framing consisted of T-frames with bulb angle frames between each row of T-frames. The hull plates were riveted to the T-frames, with the bulb angle frames in the middle of each row of plates.

The longitudinal framing method is how, today, everything from airplanes to boats to bridge girders is built. When properly engineered, it has the multiple merits of being strong, light, and cheap, and it seems to have been one of those ideas whose time had come. *Shamrock II*, built at the William Denny & Son yard in Dumbarton, Scotland, and a G. L. Watson design also used a similar system of longitudinal framing. In later years, Nat's son, L. Francis, would refine the idea (see Chapter 9).

Cap'n Nat was justly proud of the new boat, saying in later years that she was "the lightest and strongest yet built," while continuing to lament that her potential for a long racing career was cut short by the syndicate selling her to a breaker to close out the syndicate.

The rudder was made of a cast bronze frame with Tobin bronze plating. It was all sealed together and air was pumped into the rudder to reduce its weight in the water.

As was the case with *Columbia*, Cap'n Nat used steel spars with a telescoping wood topmast. The heel rope for the topmast was rove inside the hollow mast from a block at the truck.

Also new for *Constitution* were the two-speed, self-releasing worm gear winches Cap'n Nat designed to accommodate the wire rope that had all but replaced hemp or manila line for use with the loads produced by sail areas the size of two tennis courts. Like previous Herreshoff boats, *Constitution* was wheel steered; in keeping with British nautical design philosophy, *Shamrock II* used a massive tiller, which an elaborate set of blocks and tackles controlled.

headed by August Belmont, vice-commodore of the NYYC and a member of the syndicate that raced *Vigilant* in 1893, went to Cap'n Nat on November 13, 1900, and engaged his services on design number 551, the 90-foot LWL cutter *Constitution*. The contracted price was $126,000, a sum that amounts to nearly $2.7 million today. The total cost, after fitting out and sea trials, came to nearly twice that sum, over $5 million today. William Butler Duncan was selected to be the syndicate manager, a position he had previously held on *Defender* when she was the trial horse for *Columbia* in 1899. The skipper was Urias Rhodes, who had worked with Duncan as skipper of *Defender*.

Constitution was the best that Cap'n Nat could come up with. He felt that this boat was the culmination of his experience in designing America's Cup boats, and, as with the previous boats, he came up with a number of innovations that would later be used worldwide.

Possibly the biggest change was in the boat's construction. *Constitution* was the first

Constitution was built as quickly as possible, everyone aware that, as they were assembling her, *Shamrock II* was undergoing sea trials, after Watson had performed an extensive series of tank testing at the facilities of the Denny yard, where the boat was built. When *Constitution* was launched on May 6, 1901, sea trials began immediately.

Among the unique features of *Constitution* were the two sets of swinging spreaders, made of locust wood, very light and strong. The upper spreaders were 12 feet wide, stabilizing the topmast, and the lower spreaders, 10 feet wide, were attached to the masthead shrouds. The lower spreaders pivoted on the mast, and were situated below the gaff jaws, and this is perhaps the easiest distinguishing feature between her and *Columbia*, which had a single set of spreaders. On one of *Constitution*'s first outings the lower spreader on the starboard side broke, allowing the mast to buckle near their attachment point. The mast slowly collapsed, and the repairs to the boat delayed the sea trials, causing the boat to miss out on a half-dozen early races.

Constitution needed a trial horse, a boat to race against, a fast boat with known, proven performance, and the choice was obvious: *Columbia* would be refitted, her decay from electrolysis held at bay for yet another season with the infusion of cash from E. D. Morgan

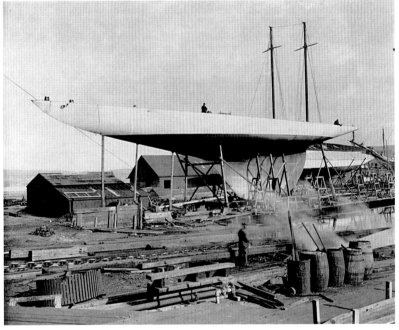

(no relation to J. Pierpont Morgan, but nearly as wealthy). Barr was selected to be the skipper and the crew was chosen on the basis of merit rather than nationality.

Over in England things were very similar: *Shamrocks I* and *II* were racing against each other in the Solent, and in late May, *Shamrock II*'s mast collapsed, with King Edward VII aboard. Neither the king nor anyone else was hurt, and Lipton immediately telegraphed the NYYC. He wanted to either substitute

America's Cup skipper
Charlie Barr at the helm
of a large Herreshoff yacht
(probably *Westward*)
with lee rail awash
and the mate making
his way forward.
Herreshoff Museum

Shamrock I and show up as scheduled or post-pone the race for six weeks. With the hurried schedule for the trials of *Constitution*, it is hardly surprising that the club vetoed the substitution request; what is surprising is that they only granted a four-week delay.

When the races finally began, matching the Cup-winning *Columbia* against Cap'n Nat's latest creation, *Columbia* beat the new boat by 48 seconds actual time, partly because of a rigging failure on *Constitution* occasioned by a clew pulling out of the jib.

Barr's sailing skills were, by most estimates, superior to those of Rhodes, and *Columbia* acquitted herself very well in the trial races, which had another contender in the form of a Bowdoin Crowninshield–designed boat built by a Boston syndicate, the *Independence*. She was of a very different type, flat-bottomed with a fin-and-bulb keel. Built with nickel-steel frames, bronze hull plating and aluminum decks, every ounce of weight was cut; she was prone to leaks, had rudder problems and, as it turned out, was never a serious contender. This was certainly to the great relief of the members of the NYYC, as her owner, Thomas W. Lawson, was not a member of the NYYC and, as far as the members were concerned, never would be. For a variety of reasons that presumably made good sense to the club members of that time, he was not "clubbable."

With *Constitution*'s rebuilt mast, she won the first three races against *Columbia*, racing in light airs and smooth water. Following two defeats in somewhat stronger winds, *Constitution* went in for a new mast, supposedly five feet longer, with a commensurately shorter topmast, but

later measurements taken on June 24 and August 23 revealed that the mast was the original length. *Constitution* again won two of a three-racer series on August 10, 12, and 14, with the third race called because neither boat finished in the allotted time.

A second, five-race series, held off Larch-mont and Oyster Bay, saw *Constitution* winning two of the races, and then the trial races began on August 31, the "real thing," as it were, previous races having been held as a sort of tuning exercise. The two boats were, apparently, rather evenly matched, as each had won nine of the 18 races completed in the pre-trial races.

And then there was the matter of the new sails. Halfway through the pre-Cup season, both of the Morgans wanted new sails for their boat, E. D. for *Columbia* and J. P. for *Constitution*. Cap'n Nat and J. B. agreed between themselves that they couldn't make two sets of sails; it was not physically possible for their loft to turn out that much work so quickly, and in the end they made sails for *Constitution*, that being Cap'n Nat's favored boat and, in his mind, the faster of the two. E. D. Morgan was not a man to take kindly to being rebuffed, and he invited the English firm of Ratsey to open a loft in the United States, their first foray here and serious competition for the HMC loft.

E. D. was, in any event, in no danger of backing the losing boat, as he was also a co-owner of *Constitution*, with J. P. Morgan.

Duncan, *Constitution*'s manager, persuaded Cap'n Nat to make the new sails of heavier material than had been used on the first set, and this certainly compromised *Constitution*'s light-air performance.

Columbia won the first race, a windward-leeward race in 7 knots of wind and smooth water, by nearly four minutes. The second, tri-angular race had *Columbia* ahead by four min-utes, 30 seconds at the second mark, when the race was called for lack of wind. *Columbia* fouled *Constitution* at the start, but no protest flag was flown by *Constitution*, so the race con-tinued, with *Constitution* crossing the finish line 54 seconds ahead but losing by 17 seconds on corrected time.

The NYYC Cup committee decided that *Columbia* was to be the defender for the 1901 race, to the dismay of Cap'n Nat, who contin-ued to believe that his latest boat was the faster of the two, and there is much to support his sentiment. Most observers agreed that Barr

was the superior skipper, outmaneuvering and generally sailing a better race than Rhodes, the skipper of *Constitution*. Barr was intimately familiar with his boat, after two seasons of racing her, and he was, without any question, far more aggressive than Rhodes. Also, *Constitution's* new set of sails, overbuilt by request of the project manager, were too heavy for the conditions, but it was, more than any other factor, Barr's superior tactics and confidence that put *Columbia* on the start line for a second America's Cup race.

When *Constitution* was helmed properly, she could fairly knife through the water. During one of the qualifying matches, *Columbia* had rounded the windward mark ahead of *Constitution*, with Cap'n Nat aboard and Rhodes helming. The designer persuaded the afterguard to tack to leeward, the first time such a tactic had been tried in a Cup boat. Under his guidance, the crew put *Constitution* through a series of jibes while flying the balloon jib, and called the course and sail trim. It was a tactic Cap'n Nat was familiar with, albeit on smaller boats, drawing on his experience with iceboats and catamarans, and it is a tribute to his skill as a racing sailor that he was able to translate what were small-boat tactics, developed on boats that sailed at multiples of the wind speed, into a strategy usable on a boat many times larger.

The strategy worked and *Constitution* passed the *Columbia* on the downwind leg for a comfortable lead at the finish.

With the contestants now decided upon, there only remained the matter of measuring the boats and establishing their handicap. Watson's design had been rule-led, just as had the Herreshoff design, but Watson's boat was, perhaps, even better at fitting more boat into the same handicap, for, although *Shamrock II* carried nearly 900 square feet more canvas, with the other measurements being very similar, she only had to give *Columbia* 43 seconds over a 30-mile course.

The general sentiment favored *Shamrock II*, or possibly more accurately, Thomas Lipton. Even then, more than three-quarters of a century before it finally happened, there were publicly stated desires that the Cup contest itself would benefit from being "passed and repasssed across the ocean," as Thomas F. Day, the editor of the influential magazine *The Rudder*, stated.

With the shooting of President McKinley on September 6, and then his death eight days later, the beginning of the races, to be held off Sandy Hook, New Jersey, was postponed from September 21 until September 26, a waiting period that hung heavily over everyone. When the first race finally began, with most of the spectators apparently fans of Lipton, the wind

Columbia before the start
on October 1, 1901.

was so light that the time ran out before either boat crossed the finish line.

The re-started first race, two days later, began in light easterlies, over a windward-leeward course. *Shamrock II* led to windward, rounding the mark with a 39-second lead, with the wind having picked up slightly to 8 or 9 knots. To the surprise of the crowd, *Columbia* was able to pass *Shamrock II* just before the finish, crossing the line 37 seconds ahead on uncorrected time and one minute, 20 seconds corrected time.

The second race, a triangular course, on October 1, was called for lack of wind, with a restart October 3 in winds of 10 to 12 knots with

gusts appearing as the race wore on. The two–gun start used at the time allowed the yachts to cross the line anytime between the guns, two minutes apart, and their individual times were taken from their actual crossing of the start line or the second gun, whichever was first. Barr luffed *Shamrock II* at the start and was behind her at the start by one minute, 43 seconds, a tactical decision in which Barr hoped to beat *Shamrock II* on handicap without having to pass, as he thought *Shamrock II* was faster on a reach. He would shadow the challenger and outmaneuver her, and *Shamrock II* rounded the first mark with *Columbia* slowly gaining, and by the second mark *Columbia* was just 43 seconds behind.

The second race's third leg, a windward beat, was where Barr hoped to catch his rival, and by a longer but faster rounding of the mark he was able to get his sails set tight faster than *Shamrock II* and, by out-pointing the Lipton boat, slowly pulled ahead to take the race, crossing two minutes, 52 seconds uncorrected time, three minutes, 35 seconds on corrected time.

The third race, held the next day at the request of Lipton, began at 11 a.m. Barr had awakened very early that day to work on the stretched-out sails of *Columbia*. Together with a sail maker named Hathaway from the Herreshoff loft he put in a fold at the throat of the gaff main, where it had stretched so much that it was noticeably longer than the gaff.

The race was under ideal conditions, a late fall day with a bright sky and a light northerly 9-knot wind over smooth water, 15 miles to the leeward mark. The two boats crossed the start line together, with *Columbia* carrying a spinnaker. *Shamrock II* was first to the windward mark, ahead by 49 seconds, and on the run to the finish the two boats stayed close, with *Shamrock II* crossing the line a scant two seconds ahead of *Columbia*. The corrected time gave the victory to *Columbia*, with a margin of just 41 seconds.

The entire series had been very close, with the margin of victory for *Columbia* totaling just three minutes, 27 seconds actual and five minutes, 36 seconds corrected, over 90 miles of racing lasting 12 hours, 18 minutes, and three seconds. It was too close for Lipton to feel he had been beaten, and upon *Shamrock II* arriving at the Erie yacht basin to be put up for the winter, he issued another challenge: next year, same boats.

The NYYC demurred, stating that, according to the Deed of Gift, a repeat challenge

Columbia leading *Shamrock* under racing rules, a position she maintained to the finish line.

Mariners Museum

required either a two-year wait or an intervening contest, effectively the same thing.

When Lipton's letter arrived at the NYYC clubhouse on October 7, 1902, members were not surprised to learn he was again making a challenge for the Cup, to be held the summer of 1903. His boat, *Shamrock III*, was to be 89 feet, 10 inches on the waterline and would be designed by William Fife Jr. Lipton was concerned about the change the club had made in the ratings system, adopting Cap'n Nat's Universal Rule as the rating yardstick, replacing the earlier Seawanhaka Rule that was based on length and sail area. Under the Universal Rule, boats with inadequate displacement for the sail area were penalized, whereas under the Seawanhaka Rule displacement wasn't a factor. The club had adopted, in December 1902, the Universal Rule, but it had earlier assured Lipton that a 1903 challenge would be raced under the Seawanhaka Rule.

With the rules now set, Cap'n Nat was again consulted, and on October 16, 1902, design number 605 was contracted, to be called *Reliance*, the most grandiose of all the Cup boats, carrying 16,159 square feet of canvas held up by a displacement of 280,000 pounds. The massive cutter was 143 feet, 8 inches overall and just 89 feet, 8 inches on the waterline. The extreme overhangs both forward and aft would cause problems. From the bow to the waterline there was a full 28 feet of boat just sitting in the air, and nearly the same amount hung over the stern. The non-dimensional numbers on both *Reliance* and *Shamrock III* are off any contemporary chart, especially the sail area-to-displacement ratio, which calculates to 53.17 for the challenger, while *Reliance*'s SA/D is an even more amazing 60.4. There are virtually no modern boats with which one can compare those sorts of numbers; overcanvassed planing dinghies like the 49er and the Sydney Harbour 18 have SA/D numbers in the 50s (if the weight of the crew is factored in), and a typical Open 60 is in the mid-50s, but those are truly exceptions. These two boats, the last built under a rule that allowed a designer to put all the canvas he thought the hull and mast would support onto a 90-foot waterline, were beautiful, fast, sailing dinosaurs. They had no reason to exist except to provide speed under sail.

Shamrock III, like *Shamrock II*, was built at William Denny & Son of Dumbarton, Scotland, a massive shipbuilding firm with

Columbia setting jib topsail to pick up more speed in 1901.
Mariners Museum

4,000 employees. They had recently completed James Gordon Bennett's luxurious 300-foot steam yacht *Lysistrata* (which featured a padded stall for Bennett's personal Alderny cow, kept comfortable with an electric fan). They were known worldwide as a builder of fast steam yachts, for private owners and industry. They had their own towing tank on the premises. Against this assembled multitude was the Herreshoff Manufacturing Company, with one designer, a four-man drafting department and about 200 employees.

Reliance began life with a contract price of $174,000 dollars, worth over $3.6 million today, a century later. The previous Cup challenge was a near thing, with many people of the opinion that the only factor that kept the Cup on its shelf at the NYYC was Barr's sailing skills. They didn't want to take any chances on losing this Cup, and so the syndicate was populated with names like Cornelius Vanderbilt, William Rockefeller, and James J. Hill, with steel magnate Norman B. Reem, railroad owner and art collector Henry Walters (his collection was to become Baltimore's Walters Art Gallery), and Peter A. B. Widener, whose Fidelity Trust Company of Philadelphia owned the White Star Line. His son, George, would go down on their passenger vessel, the *Titanic*, in 1912. Also a member was Elbert H. Gary, chairman of the board of U. S. Steel Corporation and Clement A. Griscom, one of the founders (with August Belmont) of the

pump. If the boat, when heeled as she was designed to sail, developed a tendency to lee helm, then air was pumped into the rudder, easing the task of the helmsman as the rudder lifted in the water. Similarly, with the rudder full of water its weight fell leeward.

There were two wheels, anticipating the forces being such that two men would be required to hold her on course, and a foot-operated wheel brake held the wheel as needed and was capable of being instantly released. In Scotland, *Shamrock III* had a wheel installed, the first British challenger without a tiller.

Winches, built to Cap'n Nat's design with ball bearings, disk clutches, and worm gears, were placed below deck. They were all two-speed winches, with one handle connected to a toothed-gear mechanism and the other to a worm gear, for fine tuning and getting the last bit of sheet in on the enormous mainsail. The winches could be released by simply reversing the cranking direction, and all sheets and the backstays were trimmed below by members of the boat's 64-man crew.

Marconi Wireless Telegraph Company and a shipbuilder, owner of the Red Star Line. Money was not going to be a problem.

C. Oliver Iselin was again selected to be the manager, his third Cup project, and Cap'n Nat set to work. Lacking a test tank or a team of engineers, relying on his intuitive sense, he carved the half-model of *Reliance* in the course of two evenings.

With funding ensured and victory paramount, *Reliance* was a breakthrough, if not in seaworthiness, being by any standards over-canvassed, then in the sheer number of innovations. Her rudder, built of bronze plates over a steel frame, was hollow and airtight, with a hole in the bottom. At the top of the hollow rudder post was a valve and a foot-operated air

When rounding a mark, changing the trim of the sails quickly is vital. *Reliance*'s mainsheet, made for that purpose, was tapered at each end, so that, when close-hauled and under strain, the strong central portion was stressed. When let out on a run, the lighter ends reduced the tendency for the main sheet to sag into the water, causing drag.

When rounding a mark, there was, obviously, a lot of sheet to deal with. The mainsheet was led forward from the traveler along the deck to a point some 75 feet along the deck, where it fed into a series of pulleys to send it below decks. The length of sheet on deck was done so the crew could grab it with their hands and run forward with it to bring in the sail.

The topmast telescoped into the mainmast, with its heel situated just below the waterline, inside the keel-stepped mast. As the topmast was lowered, the rigging attendant to it was stripped off by a fitting at the top of the mainmast, where it awaited the topmast being raised again. It was, like much of the gadgetry on *Reliance*, engineered to as near perfection as her 54-year-old designer could make it. No one had to go aloft to set the topmast, and it would have been a laborious process besides, with the trucks of the topmast 175 feet in the air.

The hull was made in the manner of *Constitution*, with longitudinal framing and Tobin bronze plating over T-bars to ensure a flush surface. The plating was continued over the lead in the keel, to ensure a smooth surface over the entire hull surface. The sheer strake was nickel steel, and the entire hull was braced in its interior by a series of heavy steel tubing, running at angles from the deck to the bilge, riveted to the web frames and the deck.

With 16,159 square feet of sail, the downward pressure of the mast was truly enormous.

To make the mast step strong, the area surrounding it was supported by two vertical, steel keelsons running 10 feet fore and aft of the step, with an extra frame added at the hull circumference that met the mast step.

The chain plates ran the full depth of the hull, from deck to bilge, and the mast's hole in the deck was reinforced with two partners made of steel rings, one above and one below the deck. These in turn were reinforced by four steel rods running from the partners to the mast step.

The enormous overhangs of *Reliance* were low to the water, designed to add waterline when the massive sloop was heeled, and Cap'n Nat designed the boat to begin to heel in just 8 knots of breeze. When heeled, the waterline jumped from 89 feet to 130, raising the hull speed from 13.2 knots to nearly 16.

With all the technology in the boat, and the race for which it was built scheduled four months after launch, there wasn't time for a lengthy period of familiarization for her skipper. Barr spent most of his time at the HMC shop, watching, learning, and absorbing the myriad details of the complex product of Cap'n Nat's genius.

Reliance was launched on April 12, 1903, just a month after *Shamrock III*'s launch in Scotland. The event in Bristol, just as had been the case in Scotland, was attended by huge crowds, with a brass band, dignitaries, and a flotilla of small boats full of yet more spectators.

A massive U.S. yacht ensign flag flew from the stern as *Reliance* slowly emerged from the South Shop, and less than two weeks later, she was fully rigged and making her first sea trial.

Although there was little doubt in anyone's mind that *Reliance* was the fastest of the Cup boats available, she began a series of trial races, matching against both *Constitution* and *Columbia*. The results of every race were the same, regardless of the weather or the conditions: *Reliance*, *Constitution*, and *Columbia* crossed every finish line in that order, to what must have been the immense satisfaction of Cap'n Nat.

The measuring of the two boats took place on August 17, and *Reliance*, with 2,000 square feet more sail on nearly an identical waterline, ended up owing *Shamrock III* one minute, 37 seconds over a 30-mile course.

The Cup race series was, again, to consist of alternating triangular and windward-leeward course, 30 miles long. The first windward-leeward race began off Sandy Hook August 20. Although *Shamrock III* was first across the start line, *Reliance* passed her and was well ahead when the wind died and the race was called.

Two days later, in a moderate southwesterly wind, *Reliance* was again beaten off the start line, but soon caught up and was ahead by three minutes, 15 seconds at the windward mark. Barr caught a favorable wind shift in the smoother water near the Jersey shore, *Shamrock III*'s spinnaker was launched with a twist in it and *Reliance* crossed the finish line nine minutes ahead of *Shamrock III*, actual time.

The second race, August 25, was in light airs that gained in strength as the race progressed.

Reliance got the better start this time, with Shamrock III crossing the start line 19 seconds after the second gun. Barr's lead increased at each mark; although the wind died near the finish, Shamrock III's wind died as she entered the same soft spot, and Reliance took the second race with a lead of three minutes, 16 seconds actual time.

The third race seemed at times an impossible goal. Races were called for time, then there was a dense fog and both parties agreed not to race, and the next race was called on time after another lengthy calm.

Two more races didn't even start due to lack of wind, and by now it was September 3. Finally, after waiting for an hour, enough wind filled in from the south to race. The wind picked up slightly, and Reliance was ahead by over 11 minutes at the windward mark. On the run to the finish, the wind veered east and a dense fog rolled in, so thick the committee boat shortened the finish line to be able to see its length.

Four hours and 28 minutes later, Reliance slowly appeared out of the fog and drifted across the finish line. There was no sign of Shamrock III; not until half an hour later, when the fog lifted, did anyone see her. She had missed the finish line in the fog and was small in the distance.

The Cup stayed with the New York Yacht Club. Cap'n Nat's boat, although not fully tested in the series, won so decisively there was no discussion as to the relative skills of the skipper or the unequal vagaries of the wind. Reliance was too special, too extreme, and her life was short. She was broken up the next year, and never raced again.

Lipton wrote his usual letter to the NYYC requesting the conditions for a challenge, but he wasn't to come back until the next Cup race, in 1920. In the years in between, there was to be a terrible war, a change in the ratings system for Cup boats, and, at the Herreshoff manufacturing yard, there was much work to be done on other boats.

The last America's Cup defender designed by Herreshoff, *Resolute* dips her rail in response to the wind. *Mariners Museum*

HMC Enters the Twentieth Century

Six

With the turn of the century, the Herreshoff Manufacturing Company was in better shape financially than it had ever been, with more boats and more designs coming out of the two seaside shops than ever before. There were something like 200 employees, and although the payroll had been larger in previous years, increased productivity—enabled by power tools, J. B.'s management, and building methods pioneered by Cap'n Nat—kept the yard's production impressive. In 1900 alone, 16 sailboats were built, with a total waterline of over 500 feet, a number that was to increase to over 900 feet in 1902.

Opposite page:

Rainbow, skippered by Harold Vanderbilt, crossing the line to take Cup honors in 1934.

Mariners Museum

During this time, powered vessels were a vital part of the production, although just one steamboat, an 81-foot LOA triple-expansion launch, was built in 1900, the second of the Scout class, design number 203. The next year, production picked up, with four more 81-footers built and another six steamers built, with a total of 628 feet, overall, of powered vessels. The Scout class was very successful, with eight boats eventually built, used as tenders for vessels like Cornelius Vanderbilt's NYYC 70 *Rainbow* and William O. Gay's *Athene*, a Herreshoff centerboarder similar to the NYYC Seventies.

There were winds of change blowing in the powerboat part of the yard's work. The lengthy monopoly that steam power had was beginning to diminish, with two, 20-foot electric launches built in the last months of 1901, but the real change was going to be the introduction of the internal-combustion engine. The first gasoline engine–powered motorboat was built in 1902, a 49-foot, 6-inch LOA launch named *Express* (design number 226), but in the years 1904 to 1905, just seven of the 16 motorboats built had steam engines.

Cap'n Nat didn't let the steam engines fade without putting considerable engineering effort into improving them. In the early days of the internal combustion engine, one of their main benefits was that they were much smaller than steam engines of similar output. He set to work making steam engines ever smaller, smoother, and more efficient. He drew this last generation of steam engines starting with a clean sheet of paper. They were triple-expansion engines, and the low-pressure cylinder, the last to receive the steam flow and the biggest, was placed above the two smaller, high-pressure cylinders. The connecting rod of the low-pressure cylinder was placed between the lower cylinders, with all of them driving a common crankshaft. The length of the steam engine was thus the size of a two-cylinder engine, with a slight increase in height over the more usual, inline variety.

Cap'n Nat's love for and fascination with steam engines never stopped, and it was the opinion of his son, L. Francis, that his father spent more time, over the course of his career, on the design of steam yachts and their powerplants than he did with sailboats. Indeed, his personal yacht *Helianthus II*, a 64-foot overall steel-framed vessel built in 1912 with a gasoline engine, was given a steam engine in 1919. This was the last of Cap'n Nat's boats,

Vanderbilt's *Rainbow* was built in just one hundred days in 1934. Here workmen are caulking the deck in Herreshoff Manufacturing Co.'s South Construction Shop.
Mariners Museum

whether for personal use or built for a client, to use steam. It took less than 20 years for internal combustion to completely take over external combustion.

The early gasoline engines were noisy, smelly, and lacked the reliability of a steam engine, but they put out more power for their size and were so much easier to operate and install, that it didn't take long for them to become the engine of choice, even though in the early years they were colloquially known as the "explosion engine." Cap'n Nat turned his hand to designing a gasoline engine, and it was a marvel of complex problem solving, with much of its methodology derived from his vast experience with steam engines. It was a three-cylinder engine, with the end cylinders operating as a standard four-stroke engine. The exhaust of the end cylinders was valved into the middle cylinder, extracting power from the exhaust stroke and reducing the noise.

The compound internal combustion engine was not his invention, but his design was a smoother, quieter solution to some of the gasoline engine's problems. He probably would have continued to build the engine, but he had problems with the block cracking near the exhaust valve and gave up on it before he perfected the design.

He continued to work on steam engines, and one of his last new designs, in 1905, was for an automobile, a V-6 steam engine with poppet valves (just as are used in a modern gasoline engine) in the head, allowing steam in. The steam was exhausted at the bottom of the stroke by slots in the cylinder wall, much as is done with a two-stroke gasoline engine. The engine was never put in an automobile, and ended its days powering an electric generator.

Much of Cap'n Nat's antipathy to gasoline engines was, apart from their smell, an aversion to the substance itself. This was the result of an accident that occurred when he and his oldest son, A. Sidney, were experimenting with a gasoline-fired boiler on a Stanley Steamer automobile. The gasoline was sent under pressure into a burner, with the pressurized gasoline kept in a very small tank that was constantly supplied with pressure by an engine-driven pump. The plumbing had been incorrectly installed and the tank burst, spraying both of them with a flaming fog of gasoline. They were both burned rather badly, and Cap'n Nat's hands bore the marks of his injury for the rest of his life. That was enough experimentation with gasoline to satisfy an old steam engine man, and although he continued to supply his clients with gasoline engines, he never designed

Sail makers working on the immense spread of canvas that will make up *Rainbow*'s suit of sails.
Mariners Museum

Rainbow, designed by Starling Burgess and built by HMC, was the last of the Herreshoff-built defenders for the America's Cup. She successfully defended the 1934 races.
Mariners Museum

one and, contrary to the established philosophy of making everything for his boats in his own shops, all gasoline engines were purchased outside and installed in the shops.

With the end of steam engines practically upon him, he ceased all steam engine development and design as well, and any steam engines put in boats—and there were diehards who preferred the silent, reliable power of steam—were made to existing designs.

Cap'n Nat was in the business of providing yachts to some of the wealthiest people in America, and they were people who were used to getting what they wanted. Such a person was Morton F. Plant, who had inherited a railroad and steamship line from his father and had a lifestyle that included some very expensive homes. The building that now houses the Cartier showroom in New York City, at 651 Fifth Avenue, was his New York townhouse, and he also had a 31-room mansion that, in 1905, cost $5 million dollars (over $100 million today) that was a gift to his wife.

He was a director of the Rapid Transit Subway construction company, along with August Belmont, Cornelius Vanderbilt, and others, and owned Avery Point, Connecticut, now a campus for the University of Connecticut. He sold his railway and steamship line for a sum in the neighborhood of $40 million when he reached middle age, and this gave him the wherewithal, in 1902, to pay a visit to Bristol, Rhode Island, where he contracted for an 86-foot LWL steel schooner he would name *Ingomar*, as well as *Express*, design number 228, a 50-foot launch propelled by the first gasoline engine ever put in a Herreshoff boat. He must have been very convincing in his talks with Cap'n Nat, for not only did he get a boat with an "explosion engine," he was able to convince the designer to draw him a schooner, a rig that Cap'n Nat hadn't used since 1870.

The schooner rig, he felt, was too complicated to sail, too expensive to build, and on top of everything else, lacked windward

Twenty-four crew members sailed *Rainbow*. Unlike most Cup defenders, *Rainbow* had built-in accommodation below decks. *Mariners Museum*

Nat Herreshoff's love of steam yachts is exemplified in *Helianthus*, one of at least two he owned with that name.
Herreshoff Museum

efficiency due to the windage of the rigging. However, his job was to build and design boats to the desires of the client, so the contract was let on September 13, 1902, design number 590, for $94,000, nearly $2 million today. This was the same period of time that *Reliance* was under construction, having been commissioned a month later, and it is impressive testimony to this small yard that they were able to work on two such massive projects at the same time. There was more to worry about than just two big boats during the busy winter of 1902 to 1903; the first dozen of the Bar Harbor 31 class were contracted in the month between *Ingomar* and *Reliance*, for example.

Ingomar was the first of seven large, riveted-steel schooners that HMC would build in the years leading up to World War I (with two more built in 1920 and 1923). She measured 127 feet overall, and the mast reached just four feet less than that above the deck. She was designed as a centerboard boat, drawing 14 feet, but after her first season's racing, in 1903, the board was removed and replaced with a two-foot slab of lead attached to the keel, increasing the draft to 16 feet.

Ingomar joined the NYYC racing fleet in 1903, and went about winning the Astor Cup and, in the big schooner class, every run in the club's Annual Cruise. In 1904, under the command of Charlie Barr, *Ingomar* went to England and Germany, where she continued her winning ways, despite being saddled with what many people considered to be an excessive handicap by local rating committees. *Ingomar* won 17 trophies in that single racing season in Europe. Only the schooner *America*, whose European racing career began the America's Cup series, had been more successful.

Shortly after *Ingomar's* return to the United States, in 1906, the keel was again

The first of nine Herreshoff steel-hulled schooner-yachts, *Ingomar* was commissioned by Morton F. Plant. Charlie Barr skippered her across the Atlantic to race in Europe in 1904.
Herreshoff Museum

worked on, restoring it to its previous, centerboard configuration.

Germany's Kaiser Wilhelm admired *Ingomar* so much he ordered Cap'n Nat to draw a schooner for him as well. Rather early in the process the Kaiser sent a telegram asking for his boat's measurement. He didn't like the numbers and told Cap'n Nat to change them, whereupon he was told that, if he wanted a boat, it would be built to the measurements that he, Cap'n Nat, decided. That ended the Kaiser's boat project.

The success of *Ingomar* led to more large schooners being built, but in 1905 Cap'n Nat's wife, Clara, died of cancer, after a year-long

Istalena at speed handles rolling East Coast swells with ease. *Mariners Museum*

Designed by L. Francis Herreshoff, the sloop *Istalena* was an 87-foot double-ender of the M-class. *Mariners Museum*

struggle. The death of his spouse hit Cap'n Nat very hard, and his response was to become even more withdrawn into work.

He was, at the time of her death, in the midst of another project for a big schooner, to be called *Queen*, design number 657, commissioned by J. Rogers Maxwell on December 27, 1905.

The yard had yet more big schooners in its future. As previously noted, the success of *Ingomar* inspired the yachting elite to commission big schooners, and *Queen* was followed by seven more before the fateful events of 1924.

Queen's contract price was $77,500 or nearly $1.6 million today. Like all her sister schooners, she was built of riveted steel, measured 126 feet overall and 92 feet on the waterline, with a beam of 24 feet, 6 inches. Draft, with the centerboard up, was 14 feet, 10 inches. Those who saw the boat all remarked on the smooth surface of the riveted hull. After the plates were riveted in place, using countersunk rivets, two-man teams, one with a hammer inside the hull and another with a dolly on the outside, went over the entire hull and made it fair. For racing purposes, the portholes had steel covers that fit into the recessed glass area to make even the topsides fair. Maxwell, president of the New Jersey Central Railroad and the Long Island Railroad, was himself a yacht designer. He was one of the more accomplished amateur designers of the day, but his commission of *Queen* was in the form of a short letter to Cap'n Nat saying that he wanted a schooner to race in Class B and that the rest of the specifications were best left to Cap'n Nat to decide.

Given a free hand, and with Maxwell's ample resources, the result was a boat that, in the general agreement of contemporary observers, was the finest built and best-kept yacht of the time. L. Francis Herreshoff thought the design was among the best his father had ever done. Maxwell died in December 1910, and just before his unexpected death he sold *Queen* to E. W. Clark of Philadelphia, taking as part payment Clark's 90-foot schooner *Irolita* (ex-*Istalena*, Herreshoff design number 663, built as a sloop, rerigged by Clark). Clark, apparently fond of the name, renamed his new boat *Irolita* and her final fate is noted in the margins of the HMC records, "burned Feby 1920."

The next big schooner down the ways was *Westward*, design number 692, commissioned October 1, 1909, by millionaire yachtsman Alexander S. Cochran for the sum of $118,000,

$2.4 million today. Measuring 136 feet overall and 96 feet LWL, she was 26 feet, 8 inches in beam with a bottom-scraping draft of nearly 17 feet and she carried 12,000 square feet of sail. She was the biggest boat built by HMC to that time.

She was launched early in the 1910 racing season, and with Charlie Barr as the skipper, set sail across the Atlantic to take on Europe's racing fleets. The crossing proved the occasion for Cochran to quit smoking; saddled with a habit he had been hoping to break, he threw his entire supply of cigarettes overboard once the boat cleared Newport harbor. She had been designed to race in Europe, and so the International Rule was bent to accommodate European ratings. This had the effect, as it took into account girth measurement, of "forcing" Cap'n Nat to design some drag to the keel (with the lower surface of the keel at an angle producing more draft as it ran aft, rather than being roughly parallel to the waterline) and rounded off the keel, all with an eye to reducing the rating.

The racing in Europe was a stunning series of successes. *Westward* won every race in German waters and in England won eight of nine races. The British rating system employed an additional handicapping provision based on previous performance, so with each victory, the next one became incrementally more difficult until, by the end of the season, it was impossible to win. As the season closed, Barr and Cochran had ceased to compete, content that they had the fastest schooner in the world. That winter while *Westward* was laid up in Southampton, Charlie Barr, the most famous skipper of his day and still revered for his skills, died of a heart attack aboard his last command.

Sailed back to the U.S.A. under command of former mate Chris Christiansen, *Westward* won the Astor Cup for schooners in 1911 and then Cochran sold her to a German syndicate that installed a grand piano and filled her with heavy furniture. Lying in Cowes when World War I broke out, she was seized by the British and then, after the war, was sold to a South African businessman named T. B. F. David, who raced her with great success for the next 20 years from his home port in the Channel Islands, against the best boats of the era, including *Britannia* and the various ex-Cup-challenging *Shamrocks*.

In 1910 Morton Plant went back to Cap'n Nat for another boat, with the commission

Alexander S. Cochran at the helm of his schooner *Westward*, watched by Charlie Barr.
Herreshoff Museum

Charlie Barr at the helm of *Westward*. The deck clutter suggests the crew are about to bend on a new sail.
Herreshoff Museum

taking place via the services of that new device, the telephone. He, too, wanted a boat to compete in Class B, and said as much. He wanted it to be a winner, and so *Elena*, design number 706, began, December 3, 1910. Cap'n Nat used the molds for *Westward*, but incorporated a centerboard and, as he had no need to hew to a European rating system, the keel's forward edge was deepened, eliminating the drag, and the edges of the lower portion of the keel were not rounded off. The net effect was a lowering of the center of gravity, thus making her stiffer than *Westward*, a sister ship in terms of hull dimensions but built with even greater attention paid to saving weight, as Plant wanted a boat to beat *Westward*.

Eleonora, built in 2000, is a faithful replica of the Herreshoff schooner *Westward*, launched 90 years after her predecessor. *Cory Silken*

And beat her she did. *Elena* decorated Plant's mantelpiece with silver, winning the Astor Cup in 1912 and 1913, when she also won the NYYC Annual Regatta. *Elena* finished ahead of *Westward* in the 1911 Astor Cup, but took second on corrected time. She was subsequently laid up, with the death of Plant and the onset of World War I conspiring to end her career for a number of years.

Eleonora is a regular participant in yachting regattas, including the Antigua Classic Yacht Regatta in 2003, in which she won several prizes. *Cory Silken*

Harold S. Vanderbilt was the next yachtsman to join the big schooner fleet, commissioning *Vagrant II* November 2, 1912. Design number 719, she was 109 feet LOA, 79 feet, 1 inch on the waterline and 23 feet, 8 inches beam, with a draft of 14 feet, 4 inches and a fixed keel. The contract price was $70,000, or $1.3 million today. It was Vanderbilt's second Herreshoff *Vagrant*; design number 698 was a 56-foot LWL schooner that was, apparently, too small.

Vagrant II was built to Lloyd's 100 A-1 specifications and so was heavier than she would have been under Cap'n Nat's scantling rules, and some felt the sheer line was too straight to embody the same sense of grace as other Herreshoff designs; but beauty is in the eyes of the beholder, and two sister ships were commissioned, *Mariette*, design number 772 and *Ohonkara*, design number 827, in 1915 and 1919 respectively. By 1919 the price had gone up to $133,300, which, interestingly, equates to $1.4 million, indicating that HMC was managing their expenses very well.

Vanderbilt bought the boat to race, and although it took a few years (and a name change to *Queen Mab*) for the winning to begin, *Queen Mab*, ex-*Vagrant II*, won most notably, the Cape May Challenge Cup in 1921; the Astor Cup in 1921, 1922, and 1925; and the Kings Cup in 1925.

The next big schooner was *Katoura*, design number 722, commissioned by Robert Elliot

Tod in March 1913. *Katoura* was the biggest boat ever built by HMC, measuring 162 feet overall (a size determined by the interior dimensions of the South Shop) and 115 feet LWL, with a beam of 30 feet and a draft of 18 feet. With a displacement of 313 tons, Cap'n Nat worried that she would collapse the ways if he attempted to launch her fully ballasted, so only the portion of the ballast that was external, i.e., part of the keel, was put on before the launch. The remaining internal ballast, about 25 percent of the total, was not put aboard until after the launch, when shaped lead pigs were fitted into the bilge.

The price, in 1913 dollars, was $162,400, a sum very close to $3 million today, and the most expensive boat ever built at the yard, after *Reliance*. Tod was a regular customer of the Herreshoff yard (and would commission another *Katoura*, a 92-foot LOA twin-engined motor yacht, design number 391, in 1929), and unlike many of Cap'n Nat's clients, he preferred to sail his boats himself. Described by his contemporaries as a "man of independent means," Tod, a member of the NYYC beginning in 1898, was commodore of the Atlantic Yacht Club from 1902 to 1904. He wrote a book on nautical astronomy, served for a few years as Commissioner of Immigration at Ellis Island and, after retiring from personal business activities in 1911, devoted his time to overseeing family business interests and sailing his yachts. He took his own life in 1944 at the age of 77 when Thomas Dewey, whom Tod had supported as a presidential candidate, lost to Franklin D. Roosevelt (also a NYYC member) in 1944.

Katoura was built in the South Shop and literally filled the building, in all three dimensions. The yard was humming during the building season of winter 1913 to 1914. There was *Katoura*, all 162 feet of her, filling the South Shop, and then *Resolute*, the Cup boat, in the North Shop. In between these two boats somehow the yard found the time to also build the Newport 29 footers, the first 20 of what was to become the most popular of all of Cap'n Nat's designs, the 12 1/2, and a range of power and sail vessels of all lengths.

Katoura was constructed to Lloyd's 100 A1 specifications, and used the hollow steel mast built for *Constitution* as her foremast, which alone carried 14,000 square feet of sail, and the mainmast was salvaged from *Reliance*. The rig was designed to be light and racing-oriented,

Based in Marseilles, France, *Eleonora* competes in a variety of Mediterranean regattas.

Cory Silken

Eleonora living up to her reputation as a Herreshoff schooner. *Cory Silken*

but a boat like that needed a full-time captain to properly supervise her maintenance. Tod employed a sailing master but it is safe to say that her rig proved unmanageable for either of them, and soon the rig was reduced in size.

She had an auxiliary engine, a six-cylinder gasoline engine built by the Winton Engine Company of Cleveland, Ohio, a radical innovation at the time, as all the other large schooners, except for *Vagrant II*, were built without engines. In an effort to keep her competitive, Cap'n Nat designed a folding, three-blade propeller, and this, while adding to the cost, must have helped, for *Katoura* won the Brenton Reef Cup

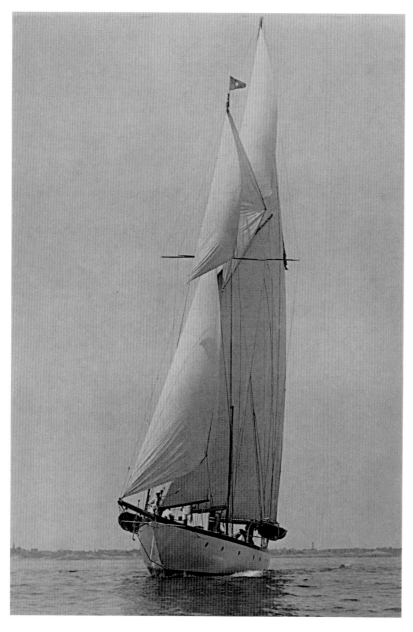

Herreshoff schooners
survived into the late
twentieth and early
twenty-first centuries.
Mariette, seen here, has
won the best elapsed time
trophies for both the
Vintage and Schooner
classes in the Antigua
Classic Yacht Regatta.
Herreshoff Museum

three times (by forfeit in 1914) and the Cape May Cup twice (also by forfeit in 1914). She was built with racing in mind; perhaps a Cup challenge had been part of the design brief, because the waterline length was the maximum allowed for a two-masted boat in America's Cup competition, but she never was considered for that role.

She made some remarkable passages, including a 253-mile day while returning from Bermuda in 1915. Sold in 1920 and renamed *Elfay*, she was sold again in 1926 and renamed *Magdalene II*, homeported in Southampton, England.

The last of the seven great prewar schooners was *Mariette*, design number 772, also built of riveted steel. She was commissioned in October 1915, for $75,000, equivalent to $1.3 million today, by Boston wool

merchant Jacob Frederick Brown, and launched in time for the 1916 racing season. *Mariette* was 109 feet overall and 80 feet on the waterline, a sister ship to Harold Vanderbilt's *Vagrant II*, and with the entry of the United States into World War I in April 1917, the racing of big sailboats virtually ceased. Indeed, the NYYC did not schedule any club racing until 1921, so Brown was not able, for at least the first few years of ownership, to race his new boat as much as he might have desired.

He finally sold her, in 1927, to Francis B. Crowninshield, who renamed her *Cleopatra's Barge II*, after his father's yacht. She was then taken over by the U.S. Navy in 1942. She survived the war only to become a charter boat in the Caribbean in the 1970s, followed by a refit in Italy in 1982. Another new owner and another Italian refit, this one in 1995, restored her to her original rig, and then, half a century after last being seen in New England waters, she raced in the NYYC's Atlantic Challenge Cup in 1997. She is now homeported in the Mediterranean.

While it was the big boats that attracted popular attention, the one-design classes that Cap'n Nat designed were very likelier an easier way to make money, with no fractious clients looking over his shoulder. Once the design was accepted, the orders would come in and, since many of the one-designs were created for the NYYC, the design's success was nearly guaranteed.

The list of one-designs drawn by Cap'n Nat's sure hand and built at the HMC yard in the early part of the twentieth century is a list of some of the best racing craft ever built. The NYYC played a significant role in many of these designs, such as the NYYC 40s and 50s, but others, such as the various Buzzards Bay classes, the 12 1/2s, the Fish class, and others, were done as commercial ventures.

The century began with the Newport 30 class, as noted in Chapter 3, followed in 1902 by the Bar Harbor 31, most of them built for Boston sailors with summer homes in Bar Harbor, Maine, or its vicinity. The first of this series, which in its first production run totaled 13 boats, was launched in March 1903. The boats measured 30 feet, 9 inches on the waterline, 10 feet, 4 inches beam, and drew a rather remarkable 7 feet, 3 inches, with the keel-hung rudder extending to nearly the depth of the keel itself. The cutaway forefoot and the graceful, nearly elliptical keel reduced wetted area somewhat, but it was the depth of the keel that gave the class its windward ability. The

contracted price in 1902 was $4,960, slightly less than $104,000 today.

In 1904, a four-man committee of NYYC members organized what was to become the New York 30 class, and that winter 18 club members each ordered a boat from HMC. The design, and the desire for a 30-foot one-design class, came about because of the success of the two preceding 30-foot classes, the Newport Thirties and the Bar Harbor 31, and it is fair to say the New York 30 class was even more successful and popular than its predecessors, and part of that reason had to do with the price of the boat, $4,000 in 1904, equal to $80,400 today. For that sum, the NYYC member who bought the boat (and they were all club members) received a boat that was ready to race and cruise, from sails and awnings to a sounding lead, two anchors, and a full set of china in the cupboards.

The yard didn't waste any time producing the boats; the first boat was ready for sea trials just six weeks after the contract was let, on November 15, 1904, and the entire fleet of 18 was in the water for the first race at the end of May 1905. The suit of sails included a main, club-footed number one jib, number two jib, a balloon jib, and a spinnaker. They were gaff-rigged, but J. P. Morgan rigged *Phryne*, his NY 30, with a Bermudan main shortly after the end of World War I, whereupon his boat was rammed by another 30, the skipper stating that

Morgan's boat, no longer a member of the 30 class because of the triangular mainsail, should not have been on the race course and thus had no right-of-way privileges.

The NY 30 measured 43 feet, 6 inches overall, 30 feet on the waterline, 8 feet, 9 inches beam, and 6 feet, 3 1/2 inches draft. The main, although quite large, was rarely reefed, which may have contributed to the first boats being subject to excessive weather helm. This was corrected by lengthening the

The waterfront at Bristol, Rhode Island, on the morning of May 3, 1914, shows *Katoura* (left) and *Resolute* (right) getting underway. At right is the steamer *Cape Cod*. *Herreshoff Museum*

bowsprit from its original nubbin of 15 inches to 39 inches. The boats, although many of them were used for cruising—and they came set up to cruise—were racing boats, and usually raced with two paid crew, of a five-man complement. Class rules required the boat be helmed by an amateur.

The paid crew, in addition to their usual salary, were also given prize money, in sums limited by class rules to one dollar for a start,

four dollars for a first-place finish, three dollars for second, and two dollars for third. In the interests of equality, crews did not race on the same boat all the time, as boats were drawn by lot before the race.

The class was an immediate success. In that first season, 1905, the NYYC sponsored nine regattas on Long Island Sound, all solely for the NY 30s. Taking into account the additional races sponsored by clubs other than the NYYC, there were 51 races for the NY 30s in the summer of 1905. A second production run of Buzzards Bay 15s began in 1905, further evidence of the design's commercial success. The success of this boat would lead to the design of the much-loved 12 1/2, of which more later.

The so-called 57 footers appeared in 1907, a class of just three boats, and they are something of an anomaly, if only because of their name. They rated as 57 feet, although they were 85 feet LOA, and 62 feet LWL, with a beam and draft of 16 feet, 7 inches and 10 feet, 10 inches. In an effort to get more performance out of them, the sail area and draft were increased and then they were known as "65 footers." They were of composite construction and very attractive, but never enjoyed the widespread success of other Herreshoff one-designs, partly due to the ephemeral nature of their rating.

The next successful one-design to spring from Cap'n Nat's imagination was the NYYC 50, designed and built over the winter of 1912 to 1913. With a 50-foot waterline, they

Eighteen New York 30s were ordered by members of the NYYC in 1904. A century later this New York 30, *Cara Mia*, is a regular sight off the U.S. east coast. *Cory Silken*

measured 72 feet overall and had a beam of 14 feet, 7 inches and drew 14 feet, 7 inches. They were conventionally constructed insofar as having wood frames and ribs. The oak frames were formed against a set of molds, standing keel-up in the usual Herreshoff manner. The 50s were the largest boat built upside down at HMC, with the limits being the difficulty of rotating the large hull.

The double-planked hull, with its large overhangs, required more than just planking and frames to maintain its shape, and Cap'n Nat had the boat built with a series of diagonal bracing straps, unfortunately built of steel rather than bronze, so rust became a problem. The choice of material might have been one of the results of the 50s being built to a price. The entire class of nine boats beginning with design number 711 was built for $14,520 each, a sum equal to $267,000 today. For that price, the owner received a boat ready to race, complete with sails. The boats were built with an efficiency honed by years of building wooden boats, 10 hours a day, six days a week. They were built two at a time in the North Shop; when the first one was framed and planked, it was turned right-side up for completion, with another boat now next to it with the molds lined up to have the frames bent over them.

They were raced with a professional crew, usually just four in number: skipper, two deckhands, and a steward. The 50s were the last of the big, expensive one-designs. In 1913, Congress passed the 16th amendment, making income tax constitutionally acceptable, and this forever changed the amount of excess money available for things like crewed racing yachts.

Despite all the attention that Cap'n Nat's bigger boats have received, possibly his most loved, and certainly his most popular, if only by sheer weight of numbers, is the 12 1/2, a design that has had nearly as many names as iterations. It has been called the Buzzards Bay

Boy's Boat, the Buzzards Bay 12 1/2, the Doughdish, the Bullseye, the Long Island Sound Bullseye, the H-12, and the Herreshoff 12. It has been produced with gaff, gunter, and Bermudan mainsails, but the hull, a seaworthy open boat measuring 15 feet, 6 inches overall and 12 feet, 6 inches waterline, with a beam of 5 feet, 10 inches and 2 feet, 5 inches draft, has remained recognizably similar over the years. It is still in production, with both fiberglass and traditionally built wooden models available.

Beginning with *Robin*, design number 744, commissioned October 30, 1914, the 12 1/2 began with a production run of 20, all commissioned

Above, left: Hauling up the mainsail on the New York 30 *Cara Mia. Cory Silken*

Above: A crew member readying the jib on *Cara Mia. Cory Silken*

Buzzards Bay 12 1/2s were derived from the Buzzards Bay 15-footers and 25-footers. Twenty were built in the first batch and sold for $420 each. *Cory Silken*

in a period of three weeks. Ultimately, HMC would build 360 of the little sloops, right up until 1943, with 10 of the last 13 boats built being 12 1/2s. They were, and remain today, a delight to both look at and sail.

The 12 1/2 has its design antecedents in the Buzzards Bay 15 and, quite likely in design number 742, *Katoura Jr.*, a tender built for Tod's *Katoura* and which has nearly identical measurements. That first run of 20 boats sold for $420 apiece, or a very reasonable $7,530 today, for a 15-foot overall, full-keeled open boat complete with sails.

With the press of work, Cap'n Nat, whose health had begun to deteriorate, sought some release. He made the first of several trips to Bermuda around 1910, staying at the Shore Hills Hotel in St. George's, with a view of Castle Harbour. Upon his return to Bristol, he designed a boat for his use in Bermuda, design number 710, a 23-foot, 6-inch LOA centerboard sloop named *Oleander*. As it turned out, the bow was too low for the choppy, winter waters of Castle Harbour, and he later said of *Oleander* that she was "too much of a butterfly" to sail in Bermuda in the winter.

At the end of that winter of 1911, she was shipped back to Bristol and sold. The new owner, in a recollection published in *Yachting* magazine years later, remembered Cap'n Nat at the helm in his "nondescript suit . . . formless felt hat . . . taking a piece of canvas about a foot square out of his pocket [to place] on his windward shoulder to protect him from spray."

The new "Bermuda boat" was *Alerion III*, design number 718, built in the autumn of 1912. Bigger, at 26 feet LOA, she was the right boat for Bermuda. Cap'n Nat sailed *Alerion* in Bermuda for 10 years, keeping her in a rented boathouse with a launching railway.

Cap'n Nat married Ann Roebuck, his second wife, in 1915; it was a busy and stressful year for the man, now 67 years old. Plagued by rheumatism, he went to New York City where all his teeth were pulled in an attempt to alleviate the problem, but the biggest, and most difficult event was the death of his brother, John Brown, on July 20, 1915, at the age of 74.

J. B. was the business part of HMC; his ability to estimate the cost of a boat, doing the calculations in his head, was legendary. The division of labor between the two men suited them perfectly. Cap'n Nat was fully aware that he lacked both the desire and the ability to be a businessman; when the heirs to J. B.'s share of HMC sold their stock to investors, the price increased nicely and Cap'n Nat took that opportunity to make a profit, selling most of his shares. The vision the new investors had was of a Herreshoff boatbuilding company, for the name was one of the business' most valuable assets, taking on military contracts to supply the combatants in the ongoing world war, whereupon they would all get rich.

Cap'n Nat did not want any part of that. One of the last discussions he and his brother had before J. B.'s death concerned taking on a series of contracts to build sub chasers for the U.S. and French navies and torpedo boats for the Russians. J. B. saw this as the salvation of the business, whereas Cap'n Nat saw it as requiring them to borrow money to expand. He flatly refused to entertain the idea.

In the two years between J. B.'s death and the sale of the company, Cap'n Nat designed one more boat for the NYYC, the NYYC 40, the last of the one-designs he was to do for the club. The idea behind them, according to the NYYC committee members, was to produce a boat that would be less expensive to campaign than the 50s, which, with a professional crew of four, could cost $12,000 a year in salaries alone, $213,000 in modern dollars. This desire for what some saw as a "sailing houseboat," with ample and comfortable cruising accommodations, resulted in a boat with rather more beam, higher freeboard, and shorter overhangs

Neith was a 53-foot (LOD) sloop designed and built by Nat Herreshoff in 1907 for his personal physician. She crossed the Atlantic at least twice, the first time in 1919. After years of neglect she was restored in the late 1970s only to be neglected again. *Cory Silken*

Nearly a century after it was built, *Neith* has again been restored to her former beauty and regularly races in New England waters. *Cory Silken*

Built in 1904, *Bambino* is owned by the Herreshoff Museum and alternates between being on display in the Hall of Boats and taking part in New England races. *Cory Silken*

Skippered by Halsey Herreshoff with a crew of nine, *Bambino* proved she could still outrun the competition when she won the 31st Annual Figawi Race. *Cory Silken*

Sometimes considered the best all-around design from Herreshoff, Newport 29s have a reputation for speed. *Comet*, seen here, was the third off the production line in 1914. *Herreshoff Museum*

than people were accustomed to seeing. The high freeboard was the result of putting a flush deck over the living accommodations, and the short overhangs allowed a larger cockpit and living area belowdecks.

Known as the "Fighting Forties," alternatively the "Roaring Forties," the 40s measured 59 feet LOA, 40 feet LWL, 14 feet, 3 inches beam and a draft of 8 feet. The original subscription was for 12 boats, beginning with design number 773, on October 14, 1915. Two more were built to the original molds in 1926.

The contracted price was $10,000, or $178,000 today, for a cruising yacht nearly 60 feet long overall. Several of the owners chose to have wheel steering, a $280 option, in today's dollars that's a $5,000 option, and there were at least two interior options.

The 40s were built three at a time in the North Shop, and put outside as soon as the hulls were complete. The first boats were taken out for sea trials, carrying the original rig

Known as the "Fighting Forties," 12 NY 40s were built for the NYYC in 1916. *Rowdy* is a recently restored beauty showing the flush deck of the original design. *Robert Bruce Duncan*

Launched in 1914, a restored *Bagatelle*—a Buzzards Bay 25—now sails out of Mystic, Connecticut. *Cory Silken*

A pair of Buzzards Bay 25s running neck and neck in a New England race. *Cory Silken*

of a large gaff main with a sprit topsail and a
very large club-footed jib with a jib topsail.
Soon, the tendency for these first 40s to
develop alarming amounts of weather helm
was discovered, and the fleet went back to the
shop to have bowsprits installed.

With the addition of the bowsprit, the 40s
became very able sea boats, and over the years
the fleet gathered a number of impressive victories in offshore races, including winning the
1924 and the 1928 Bermuda races. Both win-

ners had been rerigged as Bermudan yawls,
and the 1924 victory marked the first time that
a Bermudan main was seen on an ocean racer.

The entry of the United States into what
was then called the Great War in 1917
severely curtailed the racing of the first dozen
boats, but for that first season of 1916, the 40s
had a stellar series of campaigns, with a three-
way tie for first place in the season champi-
onship, between *Jessica, Mistral,* and *Maisie.* The
race was over a 19-mile triangular course, held

At almost 60 feet LOA, *Canvasback* was launched in 1909 with a 40-horsepower engine. Later renamed *Zara* and refitted with a 200-horsepower gasoline engine, she cruised far and wide. She is now once again in Bristol, Rhode Island, at the Herreshoff Museum.

Cory Silken

late in September as the last scheduled race of the season.

The last great one-design from the company built by J. B. and Nat Herreshoff was the Fish class, a daysailer measuring 20 feet, 9 inches overall, 16 feet LWL, with a beam of 7 feet, 1 inch and a draft of 3 feet, 1 inch. They were commissioned for the Seawanhaka Yacht Club, and 22 of them were initially built, beginning with design number 788, on January 10, 1916. All boats of the class were named after a fish, but the definition of "fish" was not one that a strict marine taxonomist would approve of. There was *Shrimp*, *Porpoise*, *Squid*, *Periwinkle*, and *Cockle*, for example; with greater accuracy there was also *Tuna*, *Amberjack*, and *Tarpon*, among others. The contracted price for this first batch was $875, which translates to $14,500 today.

With the sale of Herreshoff Manufacturing Company to outside investors, Cap'n Nat became, in essence, an employee in the business he used to own. The investors included many of the men involved in the America's Cup consortium set up to campaign *Resolute* in the Cup races of 1920. They were, most of them, familiar names to Cap'n Nat, including Robert Emmons, Junius Morgan, Robert E. Tod, and Harold Vanderbilt. The investors hired a general manager, James G. Swan, who came to the job with experience gained as the general manager of the New York Shipbuilding Company.

A harbinger of things to come was that the reorganized Herreshoff Manufacturing Company hired a designer, A. Loring Swasey, noted as a powerboat designer and formerly a member of the Boston firm of Swasey, Raymond

Weetamoe, seen here in the lead against *Rainbow,* was designed by Clinton Crane and built at HMC. *Weetamoe* also raced against, among other boats,

LFH's *Whirlwind* in the elimination races for the 1930's Cup. *Mariners Museum*

and Page. Swasey had done a lot of work for the U.S. Navy, and it is likely that the investors hoped he would bring some of that naval business with him. Swasey would go on to form the design firm of [W. Starling] Burgess, Swasey and Paine in 1920, and they would hire as one of their draftsmen a young designer by the name of L. Francis Herreshoff.

Swan, too, came with much naval experience. The New York Shipbuilding Company, located in Camden, New Jersey, had built the battleships *Arkansas, Michigan, Oklahoma,* and

Utah, and was at the time the biggest shipyard in the world.

With this high-powered array of talent and the backing of its wealthy stockholders, the reorganized Herreshoff Manufacturing Company seemed poised to transform itself from a yacht atelier to a commercial shipbuilding company. But the lucrative government contracts they hoped for would elude them, and the decline of the business would end in the near–fire sale auction of its assets and supplies in 1924.

Seven

Cup Triumphs and Business Losses

ap'n Nat would have one final, glorious moment in the history of his designs for the defense of the America's Cup. When Thomas Lipton (who, knighted in 1898, became Sir Thomas), lost his third Cup challenge in 1903 (as noted in Chapter 5), he immediately set to arranging yet another challenge.

Initially, Sir Thomas' challenge had resulted in the New York Yacht Club's refusing the offer. While Lipton's 1904 challenge wasn't so much an official challenge as it was a query, it was received with the same level of interest as a challenge. In the letter, Lipton wanted the club to establish exactly what the rules would be for the next Cup challenge. He wanted to race boats designed under the Universal Rule

Opposite Page:

Spectator boats cruising out to join *Resolute* and *Shamrock IV* off Sandy Hook, New Jersey in July 1920.

Mariners Museum

(formulated by Cap'n Nat), which would have had, among other effects, a very welcome reduction in size and, thought most observers, a concomitant improvement in seaworthiness.

The NYYC had been racing its club boats under the Universal Rule since 1903, and the Deed of Gift specified that the defending club must use (for Cup races) the rating system in general use at the club. The NYYC replied with a rather lengthy missive that boiled down to saying the club was not fully comfortable using the Universal Rule for a Cup challenge, reiterating that both parties to the challenge must be in agreement with the rules. In a sotto voce few paragraphs, the club also made mention they had noticed Lipton had towed the various *Shamrocks* to and from the previous races, when the rules specifically stated the competing boats must proceed to and from the race under their own sail. Virtually redefining disingenuousness, the club said that fair was fair; after all, the defending boat sailed to the race, and so must the challenger.

In 1907 Lipton wrote again, this time with an official challenge sponsored by the Royal Irish Yacht Club, rather than his previous sponsor, the Royal Ulster Yacht Club. He again proposed the use of the Universal Rule, suggesting the J-class boat, with its 68-foot rating, as an ideal boat. A boat of this size, said

Lipton, combined good sea manners, adequate size, and sensible sail area. The NYYC members were not convinced. Members opined, in a very well attended general meeting convened for the purpose, that Cup boats should be the fastest, biggest, and most expensive boats that money could buy. Lipton was sent a letter to that effect, which he correctly interpreted as a refusal of his challenge.

Lipton replied with a letter in which he regretted that the NYYC would not race for the Cup under its own rules. He added a short rejoinder to the flap over his Cup boats being towed to the race, pointing out the vast difference in distance required for his boats to make it across the North Atlantic to the race course off Sandy Hook, New Jersey, and for the boats built in Bristol, Rhode Island, to make it to the course.

Finally, in 1913, Lipton had a challenge accepted. This time sponsored by his friends at the Royal Ulster Yacht Club, Lipton's challenge had a difficult time on its way to being accepted. He finally gave up trying to impose any conditions on the NYYC, issuing an unconditional challenge. This was more like it, said the NYYC, which accepted the challenge and agreed, under the "mutual consent" clause of the Deed of Gift, to a race. The boats would measure 75 feet on the waterline and would be

Sir Thomas Lipton leaning on a signaling cannon aboard his steam yacht *Erin*.
Mariners Museum

built to the Universal Rule. This put them at the top end of the J-class range, 65 to 75 feet, with H-class beginning at anything over 76 feet on the waterline.

Lipton's boat was named *Shamrock IV*, to no one's surprise. She was designed by Charles Nicholson of the firm of Camper & Nicholson, located in Gosport, England. It was Nicholson's first design to the Universal Rule, and the result was a boat so striking in its design that even her designer felt that aesthetics had been sacrificed to performance, terming his boat "The Ugly Duckling." She was built of laminated wood over steel frames, with a scow-like hull shape above water that turned into a rather more conventional shape below the waterline. The lower mast stays were supported by protuberances sticking out from the hull amidships, where the hull had considerable tumblehome. Hidden from view were several winches placed belowdecks, a first for a British Cup challenger but old news to sailors on a Herreshoff boat.

With Lipton's challenge now accepted, members of the NYYC set about putting together a syndicate to build the boat. There was no question as to who would design the boat, to be raced in 1914. That honor would go to Nat Herreshoff, who had designed the previous four successful defenders, beginning with *Defender* in 1895 and going on through the races of 1899, 1901, and 1903. *Resolute* would be her name.

The club members also put together two additional syndicates, although one of them, *Vanitie*, was built and financed entirely by one person, Alexander S. Cochran, who commissioned his design from William Gardner. The other boat, *Defiance*, was designed by George Owen, a professor of naval architecture at the Massachusetts Institute of Technology, for a syndicate managed by George M. Pynchon, of whom we will learn more in Chapter 9.

The three boats, while all of the same 75-foot waterline measurement and with similar beam and draft measurements, differed considerably in their overall length. *Resolute* was the shortest, at 106 feet, 4 inches, followed by *Defiance* at 115 feet and *Vanitie* at 118 feet LOA. They all drew 13 feet or slightly more, with a beam of 21 feet, 2 inches (*Resolute*), 22 feet (*Defiance*), and 22 feet, 6 inches (*Vanitie*).

Resolute, design number 725, was commissioned September 22, 1913, for the relatively bargain price of $123,000, equal to $2.22 million

today, and nearly $1.5 million (in today's dollars) less than *Reliance*.

Resolute's hull was of bronze plating, riveted over steel frames. Her frame construction used the same method as *Constitution* and *Reliance*, with web frames and longitudinal stringers providing great strength with light weight. She was built in the North Shop, unusual for a metal boat. The South Shop had a wheeled marine railway to launch boats, whereas the North Shop had the traditional greased ways, but the entire South Shop was filled with the 162-foot bulk of the great schooner *Katoura* (see Chapter 6 for more on this boat), so *Resolute* was built in the only space available.

Cap'n Nat designed *Resolute* to carry a relatively small amount of sail in order to keep her rating low. Despite this small sail area, she carried a very high ballast ratio, 60.5 percent, greater than either *Constitution* (55.2 percent) or *Reliance* (54 percent). In the trial races held to

Resolute and *Shamrock IV* in the 1920 America's Cup races. *Mariners Museum*

determine which of the defenders would race against *Shamrock IV*, *Resolute* won in a convincing manner against both *Vanitie* and *Defiance*, although *Defiance* never was a serious contender.

With the selection trials well underway, Lipton began his journey across the Atlantic with *Shamrock IV* and his steam yacht *Erin*. This time, he was careful to sail *Shamrock IV*; in fact he gave the orders to have her sailed, as he virtually never went aboard any of his various *Shamrocks*. His mini-flotilla was halfway across, having stopped at the Azores to take on coal, when the radioman on *Erin* overheard a message from a German warship. The Great War had begun and the world had other things to think about besides sailboat racing. Not only that, with a British flag, his boats were now liable to sinking by the German navy.

The two boats stopped at Bermuda to confer with Lipton via telegraph and then proceeded to City Island, New York, arriving on August 17, 1914, where *Shamrock IV* was put up on the hard.

At the NYYC life went on, with a reduced but active racing schedule. *Defiance* was taken out of the water and dismantled, while *Resolute* and *Vanitie* continued to race. Finally in April 1917, the United States entered the war, and

the NYYC cancelled all racing for that year. It wasn't until 1920 that the club had any scheduled racing, and in that year the only racing was yet more trials between *Resolute* and *Vanitie* in preparation for the Cup challenge, now set for July.

Resolute's small sail area gave her a considerable ratings advantage, but several members of the NYYC worried that a victory by *Resolute*, which would have something like a 15-minute allowance over a 30-mile course, would not play well with either the press or the general public. To have the loser finish ahead of the winner by a quarter of an hour would defy adequate explanation. Accordingly, the NYYC Cup defense committee and the afterguard of *Resolute* set about persuading Cap'n Nat to add sail area to his boat.

He had already done so once; shortly after the end of the 1914 season *Resolute*'s canvas had been increased, reducing the time owed her by *Vanitie*, but *Resolute* continued to win races. Now, with another increase in sail area being called for, things were possibly getting trickier. Adding sail area is fairly easy, but obtaining an increase in speed sufficient to match the rating decrease is less so. A sailboat can only go so fast, that speed being determined, to a large extent, by the waterline length. The additional speed has to come from more efficient maneuvers, sail changes, and greater consistency of speeds on all points of sail.

The first race, on July 15, 1920, was held off Sandy Hook, New Jersey, in New York Bay, despite Lipton's fervent request for the races to be held off Newport. It was a 30-mile windward-leeward race in a light southwest breeze that was broken up with periodic rain squalls. *Shamrock IV* was faster off the wind, carrying 1,700 square feet more sail and with 2 tons less displacement, but *Resolute* was well ahead of the challenger on the windward leg when a sudden rain squall blew in, buffeting the boats and soaking the sails.

When cotton sails and hemp ropes get wet, they stretch, and when the sails began to dry they shrink. With the cessation of the rain, fearful of putting additional strain on the already well-trimmed running rigging, the skipper of *Resolute* gave the command to let out the throat halyard, just short of the windward mark. Poor communication between the afterguard and the isolated crewmember operating the winch belowdecks resulted in the halyard coming off the drum. This caused the gooseneck on the gaff boom to fail, leaving *Resolute* with a mainsail that hung in long sags. A crewmember was sent aloft, reporting that the gooseneck could not be repaired.

In the course of the gear failure and its diagnosis, *Resolute* made the windward mark 4 minutes, 45 seconds ahead of *Shamrock*, but with the mainsail effectively out of operation, the skipper decided to withdraw. This gave the victory to *Shamrock IV*, only the second time in Cup history that a defender lost a race by default.

The next day's race was canceled after neither boat finished in the allotted time, so it wasn't until July 20 that the second race was finally held. The second race was a triangular course, held in light, fluky airs that fully engaged both crews with tactical decisions. The challenger had a handicap of seven minutes, 39 seconds to overcome, and through fortuitous wind shifts and superior sailing, *Shamrock IV* led at both marks, crossing the finish line 10 minutes, five seconds ahead of *Resolute*, giving the challenger a corrected-time victory of two minutes, 26 seconds.

On board his steam yacht *Victoria* (*Erin* had been sunk by a German submarine during the Great War), Lipton was overjoyed, dancing a jig and seemingly quite ready to clear a

place on his mantel for the America's Cup. Race two of the 1920 Cup challenge was the first time in 33 races and 13 matches that a challenger had won by simply out sailing the defender. With the score now 2 to 0, Lipton only needed one more victory to take the Auld Mug home.

The defenders were able to count as well as Lipton, and they were getting very nervous about the next race. Losing the Cup to a challenger, even one as deserving as Sir Thomas Lipton, was not their idea of how the race should be run. It was time to call for tactical assistance, in the form of Cap'n Nat. He was in Bristol; at the age of 72, he was almost certainly content to let other, younger men fight the good fight for the America's Cup. He had done his part of the job by designing a winning boat, full of the sorts of technical gadgetry which, combined with a fast boat and good sailing, ought to win.

The 1920 race was the first with an almost entirely amateur crew, however, and some of the sailors lacked the skills of, say, a Charlie Barr. Cap'n Nat had proven his sailing skills in previous Cup races, and no one understood his boats as well as he did. To get him to the race in time, with there only being one day between the second and the third race, required fast transport, so a U.S. Navy vessel was dispatched to Bristol to bring him down to Sandy Hook.

Resolute's pedigree is evident in this action photo of her making a turn to starboard.

Mariners Museum

Alexander S. Cochran's *Vanitie* was a contender for the 1920s race but lost in the pre-Cup trials to *Resolute*. Mariners Museum

With the arrival of Cap'n Nat for advice, the *Resolute* crew set out to win a race, although he didn't come aboard. It was a windward-lee-ward race, 15 miles out and back. The winds were light, too light to start on time, and the starting gun didn't fire until 1 p.m., when the winds finally got up to 12 knots. *Shamrock* crossed the line first, ahead by 19 seconds, and half an hour into the race had a quarter-mile lead on the defender. The wind began to pick up, and *Resolute* rounded the windward mark almost two minutes ahead. *Resolute*'s ability to point higher gave her the tactical advantage on this leg, and it was a tacking duel, with *Shamrock* making 18 tacks in an effort to find

and keep clear air. With every tack, however, *Resolute* gained ground. Herreshoff's winches for the sheets and backstays worked faster and now, with the designer having given advice to make sure everything was properly used, every tack was to their advantage.

On the downwind leg, *Shamrock*'s larger sail area began to tell, and she pulled ahead, after blanketing *Resolute* while passing. Nicholson had been aboard *Shamrock* for the first race, and had joined the boat again for this, hopefully, the final race.

The 1920 race used the traditional two-gun start, with two minutes separating the two guns. Racers could cross the line anytime during

Sid DeWolf Herreshoff put his considerable nautical experience into the design for the floats for the NC-4 floatplanes. Herreshoff Museum

that two minutes, and the time difference was accounted for at the end of the race. The boat first across the start line "owed" the other boat that time. Thus, when *Shamrock*, taking full advantage of her superior downwind speed, passed *Resolute* at the finish and crossed the line 19 seconds ahead, it was actually a dead heat. But, as *Shamrock* already owed *Resolute* over seven minutes due to her handicap, the victory went to the defender, making the score 2 to 1, *Shamrock IV*. The time over the course was exactly the same, four hours, three minutes, six seconds, and the victory was determined entirely by the handicap.

The fourth race, two days later on July 23, was another 30-mile triangular course. *Shamrock* had elected to carry a smaller topsail, reducing her handicap by 21 seconds, just as she had done for the first race. With light winds again, the start was delayed until the afternoon breeze filled in at 1 p.m. *Shamrock* was first over the line, ahead by 23 seconds. The first leg was nearly a beat to windward, and *Shamrock* lost way several times as she tried to point with *Resolute*.

By the first mark, *Resolute* was ahead by two minutes, 10 seconds, but the next two legs were reaches, a point of sail that favored *Shamrock* with her greater sail area. The wind picked up, and both boats logged speeds of 12 knots or more. *Shamrock* made the most of this and by the second mark she had whittled down the lead to just one minute, 27 seconds.

The final 10-mile leg was the occasion for a squall, with both boats dousing their main topsails. *Resolute* kept her jib topsail flying and *Shamrock* dropped hers. When the wind dropped, *Resolute* set her ballooner and tacked to leeward. Now, her boat speed added to the apparent wind and she crossed the finish line three minutes, 18 seconds ahead of *Shamrock*, giving her a win by nearly 10 minutes on corrected time.

The score was now 2 to 2, the closest Cup race in its history. The effect of this was felt throughout the country. Even the New York Stock Exchange was affected, with trading described as "desultory" while everyone's attention was on the race.

The fifth and final race was scheduled the next day. The windward-leeward race was postponed for lack of wind, which, when it showed up, was too much for racing. Both boats were queried by the committee boat as to whether they agreed to postpone racing for the day. Each boat flew a flag in the affirmative.

Serendipity, a Pisces 21, is a modern interpretation of Nat's Fish class. Twenty-two Fish-class boats were built for the Seawanhaka Corinthian Yacht Club, Long Island Sound. They cost $875 each in 1916. *Classic Boat Shop, Jean Beaulieu*

On July 26, the wind died so that neither boat could finish within the time limit, although *Resolute* was in the lead when the race was called.

Finally, July 27, the boats were ready to race, although the winds were light. The NYYC

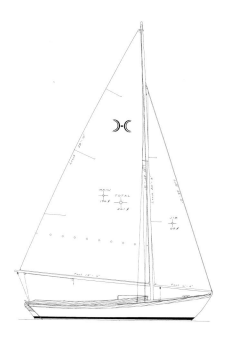

Line drawing for *Serendipity*, a modern Fish-class sloop. *Classic Boat Shop, Jean Beaulieu*

was taking no chances, and for this race, Cap'n Nat was on board his boat. Nicholson himself took the helm of *Shamrock IV*, also taking no chances. With the light airs, the start was postponed until 2:15 p.m.

Given the light airs, both boats held back their start until the end of the two-minute handicap, and after repeated tacks, *Resolute* worked her way to windward of the challenger. From this tactically superior position *Resolute* steadily gained until, at the windward mark, she was ahead by four minutes, seven seconds.

With the run to the finish line downwind, both skippers chose to tack leeward, but for Cap'n Nat, the master of the leeward tack, who had nearly invented the tactic and had

spent years perfecting it, it was the quickest way to the finish line. *Resolute* set a balloon jib, and *Shamrock*, less confident perhaps of her downwind tacking skills, set a spinnaker, after dousing her balloon jib.

Resolute crossed the finish line 19 minutes, 45 seconds ahead on corrected time. For her designer, sailing aboard his fifth successful Cup defender, the victory must have been especially sweet. His personal Cup race had begun 27 years earlier when he steered *Vigilant* to victory in 1893. Now, in another century, with steam engines nearly passé, airplanes in the sky, and sailboats built of metal rather than wood, he was still the best in the world. It was well he had this last victory, because back at the Herreshoff yard in Bristol, things weren't going as well.

Cap'n Nat, while nominally the president of the reorganized Herreshoff Manufacturing Company, wasn't really in charge. It wasn't even a full-time job, but even working part-time, he and the business manager, James G. Swan, had plenty of time to disagree. Swan's background was in shipbuilding, a far cry from handmade, custom yachts, and his tenure was short, from 1917 to 1922.

Other senior members of the company had influences on the business that were similarly at odds with the Herreshoff Manufacturing Company's past. A. Loring Swasey, with extensive connections with the U.S. Navy, garnered work for the company designing and building patrol boats, tenders, and, interestingly, seaplane hulls.

Nat Herreshoff's Fish-class boats were derived from the original model of his earlier Buzzards Bay 12 1/2s. *Cory Silken*

The first S-boats made their appearance in 1919. Designed by Nat Herreshoff, seen here sailing the original heeled over, 85 were built in total.
Herreshoff Museum

HMC produced a series of 26-foot tenders intended for the Navy, for use on destroyers. There were five built, but only one ended up actually being used by the Navy. Yachtsmen found them very attractive for their purposes, so one was used by *Resolute* as its tender and three others went to other yachts. Two of those went to the 165-foot steam yacht *Ara*, the most expensive boat ever built at the Herreshoff yard, but not designed by Herreshoff (although there is no firm record, Swasey was almost certainly the designer).

The most likely explanation for the reassignment of the tenders is that Herreshoff never designed or built boats that were built to the excessive levels of robustness needed for military use, preferring efficiency and graceful design to being bulletproof.

The larger torpedo boats were designed by Cap'n Nat's son, A. Sidney DeWolf Herreshoff, who became the company's chief designer and engineer. HMC expanded its boat business to the field of aeronautics, producing floats and hulls for seaplanes. The most famous of the seaplane commissions was the set of floats for the NC-4 seaplanes that flew around the world in 1917, and there were nearly 20 design numbers assigned to seaplane hulls.

With all the activity surrounding the Great War, naval contracts, and the shift once again to powerboats, Cap'n Nat had begun to spend increasing amounts of time in Bermuda. He was in Bermuda when the *Resolute* consortium paid a call to Bristol to engage the designer's services, and he continued to spend time there until he settled in at Coconut Grove, Florida, where he lived in a cottage on land owned by a man who had become one of

his best friends, Commodore Ralph M. Munroe, also a well-respected yacht designer.

In between his winters in Bermuda, Cap'n Nat continued to design boats, of course. That was his reason to live, and with the creation of his Fish-class boats of 1916 and the S-boats in the spring of 1919, he showed he still had the spark.

The Fish class, which had its genesis in a meeting of the trustees of the Seawanhaka Corinthian Yacht Club in October 1914, was the result of the club's desire for a club racer that would be suitable for children as well as adults, provide one-design racing at an affordable price, and provide pleasant day sailing when racing was not on the schedule.

The SCYC was in the midst of some rather hard times. The club had decided to have a boat designed and built in 1914, and the next year there was a short-lived but intense financial depression. When the order finally went to Cap'n Nat, he produced the Fish by scaling up the 12 1/2, a boat that was already proving to be both immensely popular and very seaworthy, given its size.

The first order of Fish-class boats was in January 1916. The SCYC members put together an order for 22 of the boats, for $875 each, $14,500 today. The class was also known, at least within the membership of the SCYC, as the Seawanhaka Corinthian 16, and at HMC they were commonly referred to as Design 788.

The price was cut very close, the result of a calculus taking into account the building of 22 identical boats and that HMC retained ownership of the plans, thus allowing them to sell the boats to anyone, not just members of

the Seawanhaka club. Indeed, that first price of
$875 was only good for the first order. Fish
boats ordered even a few months later were
$925, and the yard added to the profitability
by providing, for a small additional charge, a
cradle and a winter cover. By way of comparison, when Fish were selling for $925, a 12 1/2
cost $525.

Fish boats were 20 feet, 9 inches overall
and 16 feet on the waterline. They carried a
fixed keel and drew 3 feet, 1 inch. The beam of
7 feet, 1 inch gives a beam-to-length ratio of
2.92, making it a roomy little boat, and the ballast, 1,200 pounds of lead, was outside. Fish
were gaff-rigged with 262 square feet of sail in
the main and club-footed jib, and the possible
hazard associated with a large, open cockpit
was offset, from a safety standpoint, by having
the entire area forward of the mast enclosed
with a watertight bulkhead.

Later, the Fish class boats would evolve to
a pocket cruiser with the construction of the
Marlin class in March 1937, designed by
Sidney Herreshoff. The Marlin class, beginning with design number 1420, was a Fish with
more cabin, less cockpit, a head, and an auxiliary engine, although the shop specifications
on this first Marlin state there is "no motor."
Marlins were distinctively different from the
Fish class, with the cabin stopping aft of the
mast in the Fish class and extending well forward onto the foredeck in Marlins.

The design wasn't successful, even though
its daysailing progenitor was very popular. The
last Marlin was built in 1939, design number
1507, after a production run of just four boats.
Not until the Cape Cod Shipbuilding
Company bought the rights to the Marlin and

several Nathanael Herreshoff designs and
began making them in fiberglass, after some
design tweaks, did the boat begin to show up
on the water in any numbers.

The S-boats were, after the 12 1/2s, the
most successful of Cap'n Nat's one-designs.
They were adopted by the Seawanhaka
Corinthian Yacht Club as a one-design racing
class. The club's history notes that for 20 years
the boats provided the best weekend class racing the club ever had. It was a group of sailors,
all members of the SCYC and headed by Paul
Hammond, who put the idea to Cap'n Nat and
organized the commissioning of the first fleet.

The first boats were commissioned in
December 1919 and thus they didn't begin
racing until the summer of 1920. Despite this,
and due in no small part to the efforts of
Hammond, the yard was taking orders for
S-class boats at a breakneck rate, with people
buying them before anyone had won a race
with one or even sailed one.

S-boats, design number 828, were built to
the Universal Rule and following, in size, the
already successful Q- and R-class boats. They
were not, strictly speaking, a one-design boat,
but HMC built, and Cap'n Nat designed,
nearly every S-class ever built. HMC did build
one Alden-designed S-class, design number
931, in 1931, but that was after the yard had
turned out 88 Herreshoff-designed S-boats in
the years 1919 to 1931 and 95 during the company's history.

As designed, S-boats were 27 feet, 6
inches overall, and 20 feet, 6 inches LWL, but
with a much narrower beam-to-length ratio
than the Fish boats, with a beam of 7 feet, 2
inches and much more draft, 4 feet, 9 inches,

to enable the boat to stand up to the Bermudan rig, the first Herreshoff boat to be designed with the new triangular mainsail. Cap'n Nat did more than just put a high-performance main on his S-boats. He designed a curved mast to carry the 426 square feet of sail in the jib and main. Running backstays reinforced the 5/8ths fractional rig for downwind work.

The ballast ratio was very high, even for a Herreshoff boat, at 57 percent. As designed, the S-boat displaced 5,750 pounds with 3,300 pounds of lead ballast. At the end of that first, 1920 season, Cap'n Nat added 50 pounds of ballast to the forward, lower edge of the keel, beginning with design number 852, number 17 in the series.

The first 16 S-class boats ordered cost $2,450 ($25,500 today), and this was the first fleet to enter the racing circuit, having been ordered between December 1919 and March 1920. By autumn of 1920 the price went up to $3,500 ($31,400), but it was still a good price for a boat that had an active, and growing, one-design class, and one that you could also take the family out on for short cruises. The boat had two berths, but it was on the racing circuit that the class gathered a devoted band of followers. Even the U.S. Navy was a fan and ordered a small fleet for the use of naval personnel stationed in Pearl Harbor, Hawaii.

The boat developed a following and a popularity that continues to the present day, with active racing fleets on Long Island Sound and Narragansett Bay. There has not been a fiberglass revival of the class, unlike, for example, the Marlin/Fish class so the fleet that is sailing is the one made by the skilled hands of Herreshoff Manufacturing Company in Bristol, Rhode Island.

HMC was being kept alive by the construction of small boats, it seemed, especially in the business of sailing vessels. Large powerboats, including privately financed naval patrol boats, were much of the remainder of the business. There were only four sailboats with waterlines longer than 25 feet built in the years 1917 to 1924, and 1921 was significant for being the year that HMC built the first boat not designed by Cap'n Nat.

By 1923 the business of yachting was not doing well. The world had not yet fully recovered from the tribulations of the Great War and HMC needed an infusion of the sort of money only available from big yachts for wealthy owners. J. P. Morgan Jr. had always taken an

S-boat *Firefly* getting her rail wet in blustery conditions. *Cory Silken*

interest in the well-being of HMC, the more so now that it was a corporation run and owned by his friends, including his son Junius Morgan. Accordingly, J. P., who had been an active owner and racer of his NYYC 30, and who thought the class was perhaps getting a bit long in the tooth and needed rejuvenation, reckoned that the creation of a new class would build interest in one-design racing and perhaps send some business to Bristol.

He commissioned a sloop called *Grayling*, design number 892 (there were two other *Graylings* built for Morgan by the yard), listed in the records as a Q-class boat, with a 30-foot waterline and 45 feet, 6 inches overall, with a beam of 8 feet, 10 inches and a draft of 5 feet, 10 inches. The contract price was $9,250, $97,560 in modern dollars. *Grayling* was unique in her keel construction, which was structurally integral with the rest of the hull and this allowed the designer to forego keel timbers with their attendant problems of rot.

The boat failed to ignite any enthusiasm, and she was soon purchased by J. V. Santry and raced in the Q-class fleet in Marblehead, Massachusetts, under the new name of *Spindrift*, and, later, *Mary*.

There was one more big steel schooner yet to be built, the 68-foot LWL *Wildfire*, design number 891, for C. L. Harding, a Boston architect, for a contract price of $76,000, $817,600 today. She was contracted in mid-December 1922, just seven weeks before *Grayling*, and measured 95 feet overall, 68 feet on the waterline with a

Active fleets of S-boats continue to compete in New England waters over eight decades after the first was launched.
Cory Silken

Only three Marlins—a cruising version of the Fish class, with a toilet, two berths, and an inboard engine—were built. A fiberglass version was later introduced by the Cape Cod Shipbuilding Co. *Herreshoff Museum*

beam of 20 feet, 6 inches and a draft of 12 feet, 9 inches. As built, she carried a gaff foresail but shortly after she was launched Harding had the rig changed to a staysail schooner and increased the sail area. This had the result of increasing the boat's rating and thus making it more difficult to win races in the 11-boat big schooner class.

The year 1923 was not a successful one for HMC. The total sales of sailing vessels (no contracts for powerboats were let that year, or the next) was just $13,450, and by August 7, 1924, only 10 more boats were commissioned, all 12 1/2s except for one, a 6 Meter. That was enough for the board of directors. Fearing that the ship was sinking quickly, they voted to liquidate the company. They didn't seek a buyer for the entire business; they apparently wanted out as quickly as possible, cutting their losses in the face of what they saw as the imminent collapse of the enterprise. The last 12 1/2, design number 906 named *Rosinante*, was contracted August 7, 1924, and shortly thereafter the entire business was put up for auction.

What an auction it must have been. The entire business was on the block, piecemeal, although the board had agreed to sell the works in its entirety for $45,000 (roughly $475,000 today) if they could get such an offer. Failing in that, they put everything up for auction, a sale that netted $98,000 ($1.03 million today). Cap'n Nat noted, in a memoir written in the 1930s, that the prices realized were "very low."

A warehouse full of prime, seasoned boatbuilding timbers was sold, including 100,000 feet of hard pine for planking. The company had always bought raw materials in quantity, storing it for eventual use in the yard. Green

timber sells for much less than seasoned timber, and the yard bought it by the carload lot and stored it for years until it was perfectly dried and seasoned, with no possibility of warping once in place on a boat.

Sheets of brass and steel, ingots of lead, bolts of canvas, paint, screws, and tools, literally enough to build any boat a client might desire, all of it was under the auctioneer's hammer. As this dreary carrion-feast was going on, with buyers carting off the vitals of the Herreshoff Manufacturing Company for pennies on the dollar, a Bristol resident named Rudolf F. Haffenreffer Jr. arrived on the scene. He was a Bristol resident, the son of a successful Boston brewer, and something of a savior of struggling businesses. In 1931, for example, the owners of the Narragansett Brewing Company, of Cranston, Rhode Island, approached him for financial help to modernize the brewery. He soon bought the business.

Haffenreffer bought what was left of HMC, which consisted mostly of a few buildings by the time he arrived, and then, in company with a few interested yachtsmen who had the resources to assist and a desire to keep the yard going, he bought more buildings and machinery from their new owners.

Shortly, he and his consortium owned something in the order of half the buildings and a third of the machinery that once made up Herreshoff Manufacturing Company.

Haffenreffer, working with his two sons, Carl W. and Rudolph III, reorganized the company. He was assisted by Tom P. Brightman, who had been an HMC employee since his youth, and knew the company possibly better than anyone.

While this was going on, Cap'n Nat retreated to Florida for the winter, as had become his practice. In truth, he was some-

what relieved to be free of the work and duties associated with HMC. He had intended to retire with the sale of the company in 1917, and was, at best, a reluctant company president—as he later said, it was a job he "did not want and was not fitted for at [the] time of selling out."

In October 1924 the yard built *Pleasure*, design number 907, a 30-foot LOA knockabout sloop with a Marconi rig. She measured 24 feet, 6 inches on the waterline, with a beam of 8 feet, 4 inches and drew 2 feet, 7 inches. She was a centerboard boat, with outside ballast. He continued to experiment with ballast placement and its structural utilization. *Pleasure*'s lead keel served as the centerboard trunk and this kept it low in the boat while not adding to the draft.

There were other interesting features to *Pleasure*. She had a hollow mast with no spreaders, and the flexibility of the mast allowed it to bend slightly, flattening the main in puffs. *Pleasure* was shipped by steamer to Key West, Florida, and sailed from there to Coconut Grove, where Cap'n Nat lived with his close friend Commodore Ralph Munroe. The boat's long boom may have been a handful for the

Above, left: *Spindrift*, circa 1927, was probably built in 1923 as *Grayling*. Cory Silken

Above: Nat Herreshoff designed *Gallant*, a 64-foot LWL schooner, in 1926. Six decades later she won the Baruna Trophy for longest distance participant in Ocean 1. Cory Silken

77-year-old designer, so for the winter of 1925 he cut down the boom and put in a mizzen, converting the boat to a yawl, with a gunter-rigged mizzen. He put lazyjacks on all three sails, and led all lines to the cockpit. With these changes, her aging skipper could control everything from the cockpit.

In addition to his winters in Florida, Cap'n Nat spent time in Bermuda. He began to go there in 1910 (as noted in Chapter 6) and in

Totally restored, *Gallant* was on the used boat market in 2004 for $950,000. *Cory Silken*

Marilee, a New York 40, and *Mary Rose*, a 65-foot LOA cruising schooner, in the North Construction Shop in 1926 *Herreshoff Museum*

1926, during one of his visits, several of his boats were built locally to designs given them by their aging visitor.

Within another year, even *Pleasure*, despite the labor-saving innovations in rigging, had become too much for Cap'n Nat to single-hand, so he purchased from what was formerly his own company a boat that had been sitting, unsold, in the company's shop since its construction in the winter of 1925.

This was *Water Lily*, design number 982 (originally named *Limited*), and it had been built as a prototype for a one-design Cap'n Nat had conceived of, which he dubbed the "17 Foot Limited" class. *Water Lily* was 20 feet, 6 inches overall, 18 feet on the waterline with a beam of 6 feet, 5 inches and a minimum, board-up, draft of 18 inches.

This was to be the designer's last boat; he was feeling his age, at 82, and in the fall of 1930, saying he was "not reliable on my feet," he relinquished ownership of this, his last boat, to Pattie Munroe, daughter of Cmdr. Munroe.

With the end of his Florida sailing, Cap'n Nat returned to Bristol to live in Love Rocks, his waterside house located within earshot of the Bristol yard. He contented himself with designing and model making, as well as voluminous correspondence, much of it written while confined to his bed. Never a man to make much of himself, he was persuaded by his wife, Ann, to write down his reminiscences, which were eventually published in 1998.

His last design, the magnificent *Belisarius*, design number 1266, was completed in 1935, an auxiliary yawl measuring 56 feet, 6 inches overall and 40 feet on the waterline. Gracefully slim, with a beam of 14 feet and a draft of 5 feet, 8 inches with the centerboard up, she was built for Carl B. Rockwell, a Bristol neighbor and family friend, on a cost-plus contract, with the cost of construction figuring to $39,100, $525,000 today. Rockwell was already the owner of a Herreshoff boat, having bought *Alerion III* (design number 718) in 1929.

Belisarius, named after an earlier American sailing vessel of the same name (and ultimately the famed Byzantine general), was built to conform to the Cruising Club of America's measurement rule. Her intended cruising grounds were southern waters, and thus she was over-built, with bronze floors aft of the mainmast step, a backbone of riveted bronze, and a bronze centerboard trunk. She had galvanized steel frames, a double-planked deck,

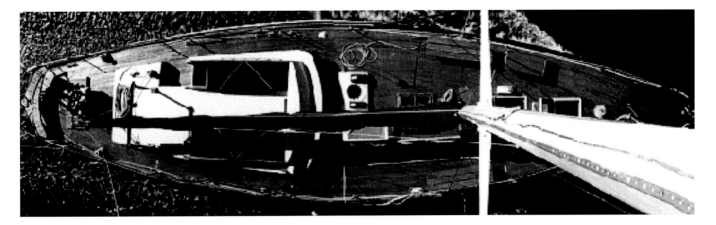

and a hull reinforced with two sets of steam-bent ring frames. The bulkheads were not structural, as was becoming the practice in other yards; as much for the aesthetics as anything, the ceiling was one, long, uninterrupted run of planking and the bulkheads were mated up to them. *Belisarius* is now in the collection of the Herreshoff Marine Museum.

Cap'n Nat's last days were still filled with an active interest in boats. From his bed, he had a mirror fitted so that he might be able to watch affairs at the yard. For his 90th birthday, March 18, 1938, he was presented with a framed testimonial from the town council of Bristol, recognizing his "sterling character and integrity," his qualities as a "just and fair employer" who had "brought renown upon his native town, placing our citizens under lasting obligations to him."

With this final encomium, Cap'n Nat must have felt whole indeed. After a lifetime of success and praise for his designs and engineering innovations, here was a testament to his human qualities. For a man whose life revolved around his work, who was often seen as distant, aloof, and distrustful of strangers, this was proof that his finer qualities had not gone unnoticed, and he was greatly pleased. Less than three months later, on June 2, 1938, the great man died at Love Rocks.

As Cap'n Nat was living out his last years, with the title of "Consulting Naval Architect" at born-again HMC, under the Haffenreffers, the yard went back to work. Within a year of taking over, the order books were full, with both the North and the South Shops cranking out boats. They were mostly smaller boats, Newport 15s, S-class, and 12 1/2s, but there were big boats as well. In December 1925, two identical schooners, design numbers 933 and 934, were built for Henry L. Tiffany and George B. Knowles. Tiffany, owner of the Richmond &

Tiffany fabric company of Providence, Rhode Island, was a relative of the jewelry Tiffany family, and Knowles was a banker in Newport, on the board of the Narragansett Bank. Tiffany's *Rosa* and Knowles' *Harlequin* were 49 feet overall and 39 feet on the waterline. The contract price was $17,500, nearly $180,000 today, which included an additional $5,000 for double-planking the hulls.

The work of Cap'n Nat's sons A. Sidney DeWolf Herreshoff and L. Francis Herreshoff became the "new" Herreshoff boats, the next generation of the Herreshoff design dynasty. Their work, and the final years of the Haffenreffer-run Herreshoff Manufacturing Company is the next chapter of this amazing American family.

Ventura's decks of Indian teak top her mahogany hull.

Ventura on a sunset sail in the Atlantic off the coast of the New York Harbor in 2001.

Patrick Harris

Eight

Like Father, Like Son: The Tradition of Design in the Herreshoff Family

Cap'n Nat and his first wife, Clara Ann DeWolf, had five sons and a daughter. Of the five, only two, Algernon Sidney DeWolf and Lewis Francis, born in 1886 and 1890, respectively, showed any inclination to follow in their father's footsteps. Cap'n Nat didn't make it any easier on them, often expressing his desire that they pursue other careers.

Nonetheless, Sidney, by the time he turned 20, had been given a corner of his own in the company's drafting room. L. Francis was

Opposite page:

In just three years Herreshoff Manufacturing Co. built 100 fighting ships for the U.S. Navy. This, the 100th, was the last off the production lines in 1945. *Herreshoff Museum*

occasionally assigned duties as an errand boy, making 50 cents a week, and spent his summers in what he probably thought of as indentured servitude, working on the DeWolf farm, which, to Cap'n Nat's thinking, was to become Francis' eventually.

In 1915, 10 years after the death of his wife, Clara Ann DeWolf, Cap'n Nat married again, to Ann Roebuck. He and his new wife went to Bermuda for their honeymoon, aboard his 64-foot gasoline-powered yacht *Helianthus II*, design number 299. Sidney was left in charge of the yard in Cap'n Nat's absence, and increasingly found himself taking over many of the responsibilities once borne by John B. Herreshoff.

On May 28, 1917, L. Francis joined the military, enlisting with the rank of ensign in the U.S. Naval Coast Defense Reserve, signing papers obligating him for a four-year enlistment. He served in the Newport area, and within a month of enlisting (at the age of 27) was assigned as the recorder for a naval board assembled to inspect civilian vessels that were being transferred to the Navy.

He spent a month inspecting vessels and was then given command of a steam-powered patrol boat operating out of Block Island. His commanding officer was Lieutenant (j. g.) Harold S. Vanderbilt, a man familiar with both boats and the Herreshoff family.

Ensign Herreshoff commanded *Enaj III*, given the more prosaic U.S. Navy name of *SP 578* for the duration, his father's design number 267, 90 feet overall and 78 feet on the waterline. *Enaj III* ("Jane" spelled backward) was contracted in October 1908 by T. G. Bennett as a pleasure yacht, powered by a triple-expansion steam engine with a bent-tube boiler. As was done by many wealthy yachtsmen during World War I, Bennett donated his boat to the Navy for light combat duty as a domestic shore patrol vessel. *Enaj III* was sold to George P. Bonnell of Stonington, Connecticut, after the war. He renamed her *Comfort* and eventually she was lost in the 1938 hurricane while moored off the HMC yard in Bristol.

During December 1917 Ensign Herreshoff was given a second vessel, *SP 56*, and he would alternate patrols on the two vessels, returning to sea on a fresh vessel as soon as he returned. After nine months of patrolling the entrance to Newport Harbor on *SP 578* and *SP 56*, L. Francis was given a shore-side assignment, this time inspecting Navy vessels and civilian merchant vessels that were under construction. Four months later, he was given a temporary duty assignment to the Experimental Station at the submarine base at New London, Connecticut. Here he worked on the design of torpedo and submarine shapes.

Right, and the next six photos: In the early 1900s, up to America's entry into World War I in 1917, Herreshoff Manufacturing Co. built a series of steam boats for private owners that were acquired by the Navy in 1914. Known as SP-boats they ranged in size from 58 feet to 83 feet. Pictured here are: USS *Sea Hawk* (SP-2365), USS *Herreshoff 309* (SP-1218), USS *Stinger* (SP-1252, originally *Herreshoff 312*), USS *Snark* (SP-1291), USS *Ellen* (SP-1209, built as *Herreshoff 314*), USS *Lynx II* (SP-730), and USS *Herreshoff 306* (SP-1841). *National Archives*

Francis' enlistment in the Navy did not meet with his father's approval. Cap'n Nat, while not quite a conscientious objector, had no affection for the military, and taking military contracts was a sore point between him and his late brother that had caused difficulties several times. Yet, Cap'n Nat could have seen it coming. Francis had already served one enlistment in the Rhode Island State Militia and, during his three years at Rhode Island State College (where he studied agriculture at the behest of his father), he participated in military training exercises and was on the rifle team, where he was awarded an "expert" medal.

There was never any doubt in Francis' mind that he was going to be a naval architect, despite his dalliance with the military. He noted, in a letter to his commanding officer at New London, that he had studied naval architecture since childhood "under the most favorable conditions," a modest description of an apprenticeship served under the world's leading designer of watercraft.

While Francis was in the Navy, brother Sidney was designing boats in addition to keeping an eye on the functioning of HMC. In 1917, he designed a series of five, 40-foot motorboats, design numbers 324 to 328, for $49,750 each, nearly $716,000 today. He also designed several launches the Navy used to

recover spent torpedoes at the Newport torpedo testing facility.

When Francis was relieved from active duty status on March 14, 1919, he returned home to Bristol. He didn't stay long, though. In 1922, he moved out for good, taking up residency in rooms above a garage owned by Charles B. Rockwell, a long-time Herreshoff

client. In 1924, when HMC was on the auction block and it seemed that the famous business would soon be nothing more than a memory, Rockwell stepped in and asked both Francis and Sid to join him in forming a new business, with them as designers. They both turned him down; Sid had been made chief engineer of HMC in 1918 and expected to continue in that capacity with the Haffenreffers, and Francis had by then moved to Provincetown and then Boston, where he worked for the design firm of Burgess, Swasey and Paine until 1925, when he moved to Marblehead, Massachusetts.

Besides his design work (which is covered in Chapter 9), Francis was in demand as a crewmember. In 1921, he crewed on races at the Seawanhaka Yacht Club on the 6 Meter *Jeanie*, a Starling Burgess design, with owner Frank C. Paine and Nicholas Potter, who was also working at HMC as a designer, lending a hand to Sid Herreshoff. *Jeanie* was one of the four 6 Meters sent to England to compete in the first International 6 Meter races, at that time the only 6 Meters in the country. Together with the other three boats, *Montauk*, *Grebe*, and *Sheila*, the boats were shipped June 25, 1921, on the Wilson Line's *SS Francisco*,

which made a special stop at the Solent to drop off the boats. The crew sailed across on the *SS Aquitania*, meeting their boats for the summer race series.

The American sailors didn't cover themselves with glory, losing to the U.K. sailors 117 to 88 in the six-race series, and *Jeanie* never finished better than fourth place. The race was significant in one other way. *Sheila*, designed

by Burgess but built at HMC, design number 861, was the first sailing yacht to come out of the yard not designed by Cap'n Nat. *Sheila* never made it back across the ocean to her home waters. Built for Paul Hammond, she was sold to British owners who continue to sail her today.

Hammond was to figure prominently in Francis' life, as a member of the syndicate that

commissioned Francis' J-class *Whirlwind*, built for the 1930 Cup challenge. He also owned the LFH-designed 71-foot ketch *Landfall*, LFH design number 49, also built in 1930. (There is more information on these boats in Chapter 9.) Although not a Herreshoff boat, Hammond's Burgess-design schooner *Niña* is perhaps his most well-known boat. Built in 1928, she won the transatlantic race from Sandy Hook to Santander, Spain, the year she was launched, and created something of a stir when she appeared with her staysail rig and Bermudan main, becoming the first boat to race across the Atlantic with the radical, three-sided sails.

At the Haffenreffer-owned HMC, Sid proved an able manager and an innovative designer. He lived next door to his father's house, Love Rocks, with his daughter Agnes Mueller, named after Karl Friedrich Herreschoff's mother, liaised with Corporal Eschoff in the seventeenth century. Sid was the man in charge, although his retiring nature made that a difficult role for him. In the absence of his father, Sid was the person whom everyone in the shop went to. The problem was that Sid just wasn't endowed with the competitive nature that his father and L. Francis had.

Kelpie, a Fishers Island 31,
being loaded onto a
trailer outside the East
Construction Shop in 1930.
Herreshoff Museum

Sid was given 20 percent of his father's shares in HMC, in an effort, according to Cap'n Nat, "to stimulate him with the hopes of his taking more interest in the control [of HMC]." Part of Sid's problem was one he shared with his brother: their father had never had much faith in either of them. In a letter to L. Francis, Cap'n Nat said that after J. B. died "it was obvious to me that not one of my boys had the ability to run the shops," and that he might have continued to superintend the work but "could not find anyone to take your Uncle John's place."

Sid would go on to design most of the powerboats HMC built in the 1930s, and his work with sailing vessels produced many memorable designs. Although he was not as prolific as his father, an exact count of his designs is somewhat more difficult to come up with. He was a reticent, almost shy man, his designs were not marked as such on the company's construction records, but he still had a considerable reputation as a designer, continuing his career after the final dissolution of HMC in 1946.

He designed the "wishboom" rig, a split boom for a loose-footed mainsail that produced a good sail shape, with the tension on the clew, and was light. The rig was used on several of Sid's designs, including the *Frost Fish*, design number 1267, a dinghy he designed in 1934 for the growing sport of racing small, open boats during the winter, given the nickname "frostbiting" by newspaper writers. Sid was a frostbiting devotee, and both he and Potter designed boats for the sport.

The Fishers Island 31, in 1929, was designed by Sid with inspiration from his father's *Alerion III*, the third of Cap'n Nat's personal boats to bear the name, design number 718, in 1912, and the smallest at 21 feet, 9 inches LWL. The first of the series was *Savage*, design number 1153, built for Thomas W. Russell for $16,000. That was just before the dark days of the Great Depression; that sum in today's dollars is nearly $172,000, a decent sum of money then as now.

The FI 31, with its 31-foot waterline, was more than just a stretched-out *Alerion III*, although Sid began the design by expanding the scale of his father's boat. He added a full keel, considerably adding to the draft, going from 30 inches to 6 feet, 1 inch, and the length overall was similarly increased, from 26 to 44 feet with graceful overhangs fore and aft. *Alerion III*'s beam of 7 feet, 7 inches was proportionally

increased to 10 feet, 7 inches. Not just a racer, the FI 31 had accommodations suitable for short cruises, with one making a circumnavigation 30 years after it was commissioned.

HMC built an even dozen of the Fishers Island 31s, but the introduction of this design, most of which were purchased by the "summer people" of Fishers Island, was ill-timed. The first boat was contracted September 27, 1929, just a month before the day that the stock market began the precipitous fall that heralded a decade of financial hardship. Even the wealthy were affected; admittedly not to the extent felt by those who weren't regular customers of yacht designers, but the Fishers Island 31, with a price that was roughly equivalent to eight times the average annual income, was still a victim. Instead of the boats becoming a design that would keep the production lines full at Herreshoff Manufacturing Company, the production stopped just one year after it began with design number 1190, the twelfth of the series.

With sales of larger boats compromised by the economic malaise, smaller and cheaper boats became a design priority. In Europe, the various so-called "Meter classes" were becoming popular, and the designs were gaining in familiarity, if not popularity, here, through the efforts of L. Francis. He wrote about the boats

in *The Rudder* and *Yachting*, and designed meter-boats as well.

Cap'n Nat had used one-off designs to test new concepts or assist his clientele in making decisions on their new boat, and Sid used this proven concept in design number 1204, *Silver Heels*, built in 1931 as a "company boat" (as opposed to a boat built for a family member) to experiment with the general design philosophy mandated by the "square-meter" classes. This, generally speaking, was a hull with a low beam-to-length ratio and a sail plan that was easy to handle since the hull was easily driven. *Silver Heels'* graceful overhangs gave the design an overall length, 32 feet, that was more then 50 percent longer than the waterline length of 20 feet. Even calculating the waterline length, the beam-to-length ratio was low, with a beam of just 5 feet, 6 inches. Strictly speaking, the boat was not a meter-boat, but it shared design philosophy, if not genetic material, with the 22-square-meter class.

Silver Heels originally came with a jib and Bermudan main of 225 square feet, but within four years Sid had put one of his "wishboom" rigs on it, and in 1938 the boat was sold, for $1,500 (nearly $20,000 today).

A year after *Silver Heels'* debut, HMC began to advertise their new 34-foot LOA sloop,

The Novara car, designed and built by Sidney Herreshoff, was the only one of its kind. Fast for the time, it was wrecked at a dirt-track race in 1922.

Herreshoff Museum

designed by Sid as a smaller, cheaper craft for those sailors desirous of getting out on the water but no longer able to purchase boats in the manner to which they had become accustomed in the more flush times of the Roaring Twenties. This was the boat, at first known only as a "23 foot waterline sloop," that was to become the Fishers Island 23, later known as the H-23. The FI 23's lineage came from *Alerion III* via *Silver Heels*, but with a greater beam, at 7 feet, and slightly more draft, at 4 feet, 6 inches.

The first production run of eight boats began with design number 1212, with most of that first fleet delivered by early summer of 1932, for a contracted price of $2,750 ($33,250 today). Eventually there were 13 full-keel FI 23s, with a fourteenth, design number 1225, built with a centerboard that reduced the draft to 2 feet, 11 inches.

At least one of the FI 23s went to a former FI 31 owner, and it was the formation of a class at Fishers Island that gave the boat its name. The name evolved to H-23 as boats were purchased by sailors living elsewhere.

The H-23 lacked any accommodations for cruising, as might be imagined considering the size, and thus Sid set to work, with the assistance of Nick Potter, on design number 1227, described in company records as a "forty-square meter type" but known as a Northeast Harbor 30 for what was identified in company records as the three-boat fleet's Maine destination and, in the manner of all Herreshoff boats, the waterline length.

Proportionally, the Northeast Harbor 30s were even more slender than *Silver Heels*, the last meter-inspired boat to come from Sid's drawing board. The intention was the same, with the narrow hull allowing the boat to be easily driven. The Northeast Harbor 30 was 47 feet, 2 inches overall, with a beam of 7 feet, 10 inches and a draft of 5 feet, 6 inches.

Northeast Harbor 30s sold for $8,000—equivalent to $108,000 today—and like the H-23 they were designed to be built to an attractive price. One of the results was that both designs were built with a single layer of planking on the hull. The standard practice with Cap'n Nat's designs had always been to use two layers of hull planking, fitted so tightly that caulking was not required. This gave a smooth, fast finish, and with two layers of planking, was watertight once the planks "took up" after launching. Both the Northeast Harbor 30s and the H-23s were built with a single layer of planking, which roughly halved the time and materials bill for the hull. Fitted with the sort of precision

expected in a boat built at the Herreshoff yard, the planks were not caulked and the hull was perfectly fair.

Unfortunately, the hulls also leaked. With only one layer of planking, the boat "worked," racking due to strain in a seaway and, with the planking swelling and shrinking as the boats were taken out of the water, the stresses were sometimes so severe that frames broke.

In 1934, Sid designed a boat for his family. Called *Velita*, the 16-foot LOA centerboard sloop sparkled with unique features, including his wishboom mainsail and a jib that incorporated a forestay. The halyards did double duty as shrouds, and a continuous line that was rove to the cockpit, rather than a tiller, controlled the rudder. With a waterline length of 15 feet and a beam of 5 feet, 8 inches, the open daysailer was just the sort of boat his father would have made, an easily rigged small boat that also functioned as a test bed for ideas. *Velita* was not given a design number. The boat was built during a time when the biggest boat in the shop was W. Starling Burgess' America's Cup defender, the J-class *Rainbow*. There were a number of dinghies built in 1934, including 22 Frostbite dinghies during the month of September.

Motor yachts were an important part of the business during the Depression, but sailing vessels kept the company solvent. Between

1930 and 1939, there were 379 sailing vessels contracted. Even though nearly 180 of these were various permutations of the beloved 12 1/2, with nearly three dozen Frost Fish dinghies added in, there were also some major commissions, including three America's Cup boats, *Enterprise*, *Weetamoe*, and *Rainbow*, mentioned above. While these J-class boats were not Herreshoff-designed, together they accounted for more than 373 feet of yacht, built on a "cost-plus" contract.

In 1935, Sid went to work on a 13-foot, 1-inch LOA wishboom-rigged open boat (referred to in company records as a "wishbone") called the Amphi-Craft, an allusion to the trailer, also designed by Sid, that could be ordered with the boat. The concept was not a new one; boat trailers had been developed in the 1920s by scow sailors in the Great Lakes region, and in 1931 *Rudder* magazine editor William Crosby designed and published plans for a "trailer-class" boat he named the *Snipe*.

The first Amphi-Craft was design number 1276. Cars were narrower then, and the beam was just 4 feet, 9 inches, with the wire-spoked wheels and their motorcycle fenders coming up nearly to the gunwales. And motorcycle fenders they truly were; the wheels and fenders were purchased from the Indian Motorcycle Company, ordered from their factory in

A variety of craft in the Hall of Boats at the Herreshoff Museum, including *Torch*, a Fishers Island 31, in the center. *Herreshoff Museum*

Springfield, Massachusetts. The rest of the trailer was done in true boatyard fashion, with the frame made of stem-bent oak frames.

Unlike most of the Herreshoff boats, which were carvel planked, with the edges of the plank butting smoothly to each other, the Amphi-Craft was of lapstrake construction, with each plank overlapping the one below. The mast broke down into two sections that would fit within the boat for trailering and the rudder pivoted to allow the boat to navigate the shallow water near launching sites. The centerboard was long and rather thin, with a straight leading edge to come up flush with the hull when fully raised.

The Amphi-Craft, with its single, wish-boom main, was easy to sail. The shape of the sail was controlled by the snotter, a line from the clew, where there was block giving a 2 to 1 advantage, leading to the base of the mast. The mainsheet controlled the angle of the sail in the usual manner.

You could order an Amphi-Craft with an outboard motor, and a third of the 15 boats sold were ordered without a trailer, a $50 option. Price with a trailer was $560, roughly $7,500 today, which was about four months' work at the average wage, if you had a job. It was 1935 and unemployment was still at 20 percent, down from the 25 percent during the

worst of the Great Depression in 1932, but still not a climate favoring massive boat-buying by the working public.

It was a notable effort. The 12 1/2 was selling for nearly $900 at that time, and it didn't come with a trailer. But the Amphi-Craft never caught on, despite what, for the Herreshoff Manufacturing Company, was an advertising blitz.

Sid's design work on sailing vessels in the 1930s was notable, but the majority of the sailboats to come out of the yard were not of his design. He did, however, design many of the motor yachts of the 1930s, although the total number of boats built during that decade was not large, with just 20 boats ordered.

The motor yacht *Stroller*, design number 388, was designed by Sid and contracted in 1929. Her design was used for a later boat, *Ariel II*, built in 1931, the only motor yacht for that year. *Stroller* and *Ariel II* were each 46 feet, 9 inches overall and 46 feet on the waterline. *Stroller*'s beam was increased by an inch on *Ariel II*, to 10 feet, 6 inches and the draft increased, from *Stroller*'s 2 feet, 9 inches to *Ariel II*'s 3 feet, 1 inch.

Stroller was a twin-engine, twin-screw vessel, powered by two, six-cylinder Sterling Petrel gasoline engines. She was built for C. D. Rafferty Jr. for a contracted price of $24,500, a sum equivalent to $163,000 today. Things were slowing down; there were just three boats

was covered with a streamlined roof, open on the sides. From the vantage point afforded by its raised position, the skipper could look at those seated in the open, forward cockpit, with the flat-paned windshield affording at least some measure of protection from the wind. The aft cockpit had a windshield/roof combination very similar to that of the pilothouse. Powered by two Sterling Petrel gasoline engines, it was built for Marshall Sheppey of Toledo, Ohio, who paid $23,000, $304,000 in today's dollars, for this, the last civilian boat of any size built at the Herreshoff yard.

In the years leading up to the war, there weren't many sailboats built either, mostly 12 1/2s, including two built for the Haffenreffers. Design number 1506, another of Sid's *Silver Heels*, was built in 1939 for J. Peter Geddes II, who christened his new boat *Silver Heels II*. The price was $2,200, $29,000 today.

With war looming, military contracts revived the company. Beginning in June 1941, with four, 97-foot LOA minesweepers for the U.S. Navy, HMC began to design and build boats for war. Between June 1941 and January 1945, when the last military boat was built, 525 boats were built for the U.S. Army and the navies of the United States, Britain, and Russia.

There were still two sailboats to be built, both of them after World War II ended in September 1945. Design number 1519 was *Sea Spider*, a 30-foot catamaran, designed by Sid for Cornelius Crane and ordered through Sparkman & Stephens. The price was $3,000 (just over $28,000 today), and the end was

World War II saw Herreshoff Manufacturing Co. producing a large number of boats for the U.S. Navy. Among them were eight 71-foot Vosper PT boats. Herreshoff Museum

Herreshoff Manufacturing Co. built two YMS minesweepers, both 130-feet LOA, for the Navy during World War II. Herreshoff Museum

listed that year, although a number of boats begun earlier were launched in 1929.

Ariel II, design number 393, was a sister ship of *Stroller* with a small increase in beam and draft. She was the only motor yacht built that year, and it is perhaps indicative of the volatile nature of the economy in 1931 that the contract listed the prices as "cost plus." She was built for William E. Woodard in the East Shop.

The motorboat part of the business slowly ticked over as the Depression continued. Military contracts, with the first ones beginning in June 1941, were of no help in the late 1930s. There were just two large, private motor yachts built after *Ariel II*: *Avoca*, design number 408, a 69-foot LOA twin-engine vessel designed by Sparkman & Stephens and Sid's *Sheerness*, in October 1939, design number 410. *Sheerness*, 52 feet, 6 inches LOA, 51 feet LWL with a 12-foot beam and drawing 3 feet, had three open cockpits. The midships pilothouse

nigh. Design number 1520, an order for 25 of the 12 1/2s, was never fulfilled, and then, in February 1946, design number 1521, the last boat of the Herreshoff Manufacturing Company, was built. It was a Fishers Island 31, built for Navy veteran Robert N. Bavier Jr., who would go on to be editor and then publisher of *Yachting* magazine and skipper the 12-meter *Constellation* to victory in 1964. Bavier paid $14,500 for his FI 31, equal to $137,000 today.

With the closing of HMC, Sid continued to work as a naval architect. When the plans for the 12 1/2 were sold to the Cape Cod Shipbuilding Company of Wareham, Massachusetts, he helped in their redesign, resulting in the boat now known as the "Herreshoff Bullseye."

In 1955 he designed the Gemini for Cape Cod Shipbuilding, a fiberglass, twin-centerboard sloop measuring 16 feet LOA, 14 feet, 9 inches LWL, and with a beam of 5 feet, 7 inches. With the board up it drew only 7 inches, in-creasing to 3 feet, 4 inches for windward work. The planing hull displaced 440 pounds, with a total sail area of 140 square feet. It was self-righting, with the aid of an enclosed flotation chamber and foam sections under the decks. Cape Cod built 150 of them, with a selling price of $5,525, or $38,000 today.

In 1971, Sid founded the Herreshoff Maritime Museum, in Bristol, Rhode Island, on the site and used some of the buildings of the Herreshoff Manufacturing Company.

While Sid was working at HMC, his brother L. Francis had his own yacht designing business in Marblehead, Massachusetts, and the story of his boats fill the next chapter.

As part of a contract for the U.S. Navy, Herreshoff Manufacturing Co. built twenty-two 103-foot APCs. *Herreshoff Museum*

Nine

L. Francis Herreshoff: The Torch is Passed

I t didn't take long for L. Francis Herreshoff to tire of working for someone else. His design career, outside of his father's company, began with his working for W. Starling Burgess in Provincetown, Massachusetts, in 1920. When Burgess and two partners started the design firm of Burgess, Swasey and Paine in Boston a few years later, L. Francis joined them.

It was an elite gathering of designers and a high-octane office, with the three designers bringing complementary skills. A. Loring Swasey had been employed at Herreshoff Manufacturing Company in 1917 as their chief designer, but he only stayed there until 1923, when he joined forces with W. Starling Burgess and Frank Paine. While working

Opposite page:

Silver Heels was employed by Herreshoff Manufacturing Co. for demonstration purposes as well as development of future designs such as the Fishers Island 23 and the Northeast Harbor 30s.

Herreshoff Museum

at HMC, Swasey had designed *Ara*, design number 377, a 165-foot motor yacht that had the distinction of being the most expensive boat ever built at the yard. Given the rarified atmosphere occupied by expensive boats at HMC, this was saying something. The contract price was $230,000 in 1921 dollars, or nearly $2.4 million today. Paine's list of boats includes the J-class *Yankee*, an America's Cup contender for the 1930 race, and of Burgess it could be said he had yacht designing in his blood, just as L. Francis did. Father Edward Burgess designed the winning Cup boats *Puritan* (1885), *Mayflower* (1886), *Volunteer* (1887), and *Vigilant* (1893) and son W. Starling designed the J-class Cup boats *Enterprise* (1930), *Rainbow* (1934), and *Ranger* (1937).

While in Boston, L. Francis lived for the winter of 1924 to 1925 on a mastless boat moored in the Charles River. During his time as a draftsman with Burgess, Swasey and Paine, L. Francis invented the tangs that nearly all

The 1930s J-boat *Whirlwind*, while designed by L. Francis Herreshoff, was built at the Lawley yard in Neponset, Massachusetts. *Mariners Museum*

boats now use to attach the stays to the mast, but perhaps the most significant boat he designed during his time there turned out to be the predecessor of *Tioga*, the 57-foot ketch that was one of his most beautiful designs. The original was *Joann*, a 49-foot, 11-inch overall gaff schooner, designed for Edward Dane, and was design number 257 at Burgess, Swasey and Paine. Dane liked the boat and the designer, and returned to L. Francis in 1931 for a larger version, which became *Tioga*, LFH design number 50, built in the Britt Brothers yard of West Lynn, Massachusetts, and launched finally in 1936.

In 1925, Burgess left the firm and fairly soon thereafter so did L. Francis, who in 1926 moved to 20 Lee Street in Marblehead, Massachusetts.

His relationship with his father began to deepen (or at least exist) as they started to exchange regular letters, in which Francis (as he was addressed by his father) told of his new designs, observations of boats, and lengthy discussions on ratings rules. Whenever L. Francis was mentioned in a magazine or newspaper, he would send a clipping to his father, who began to take obvious pride in his son's growing status as a yacht designer.

The correspondence began in March 1925, more than five years after L. Francis had left Bristol, when Cap'n Nat saw a photograph of his son in a Boston newspaper. It was the day after the elder Herreshoff turned 77 when he decided to write, adding in a postscript that he "would be pleased to have a letter" in return.

Cap'n Nat had never been one to display feelings openly, and his relationship with L. Francis was colored by his son's mild dyslexia. Fearing that L. Francis was somehow not bright enough, he had laid out a career for him as the family's "farmer," sending him to college to study agriculture, but as previously noted that didn't last. L. Francis knew he wasn't cut out to be a farmer, and instead followed his own creative impulses as a yacht designer. Neither he nor his brother Sid were encouraged in this, and it wasn't until he began to receive acclaim that his father took paternal notice of him.

By 1925, L. Francis was cited by *Yachting* magazine as the best designer of R-class boats in Massachusetts Bay, which meant that his were among the best anywhere. The most successful of these early R-class boats was *Yankee*, in 1924, done while in Boston. *Yankee* was built at the Britt Brothers yard for Charles A. Welch Jr. using longitudinal construction, with all framing and supports running fore and aft, the first boat to use the method. With some later improvements, he patented the idea in 1929. This was a modified form of the longitudinal and web frame construction Cap'n Nat used on *Constitution* in 1900.

Once in business under his own name, L. Francis set about designing more racing boats, and his R-class *Live Yankee*, the most expensive R-class ever built, was commissioned by Welch and launched in 1927. Much of that cost can be attributed to the innovative aspects of the design and the problems with getting things done per the designer's wishes. Cap'n Nat, commenting on the blueprints his son sent him, said the boat "bristles all over with new and original ideas." Incorporating a rotating mast, a luff spar for the double-luffed headsail, streamlined deck edges for sailing with the lee rail under, adjustable spreaders, and a rudder that was actually part of the keel, effecting steering by flexing, it was the most radical design of its time. It wasn't all completely new, at least to the designer. Aspects of the rotating mast had been worked out in an iceboat that L. Francis had designed two years previously. She was also a "lead mine," with a ballast ratio of 80 percent. Despite all the innovations, her racing career was not equal to that of the earlier *Yankee*.

That said, the year *Live Yankee* was launched she won the New York Yacht Club's R-Class Cup, finishing first in all three races of the series, and skippered by Welch, a member of the Eastern Yacht Club. The wins didn't come until after Welch and his boat spent the first part of the season either trailing the fleet or in the yard doing repairs.

And then there were the ratings committees. Puzzled by the boat, the problems began when they outlawed the double-luff headsails before the boat was even launched.

Ticonderoga, a 72-foot clipper-bow ketch designed by L. Francis Herreshoff in 1937, broke many records for speed and performance. *Cory Silken*

Built for Harry Noyes, *Ticonderoga* is considered to be L. Francis Herreshoff's crowning achievement. *Cory Silken*

The Herreshoff Marine Museum on Narrangansett Bay, Rhode Island, opened in 1971. It is the custodian of Herreshoff boats, as well as a library of yachting memorabilia and the America's Cup Hall of Fame.
Herreshoff Museum

Despite the difficulties the owner had with ratings committees, L. Francis was not deterred in his pursuit of new ideas. To his father he wrote, "History shows us that almost all improvements in mechanical devices have been condemned by people imbued with tradition. Note, the Steam railways, screw propellers, automobile and aeroplane. . . . I expect to bring out several new things in the next few years, and am not going to be discouraged by criticisms."

In 1928, he designed the M-class *Istalena*, measuring 87 feet overall, for longtime Herreshoff client and NYYC member George M. Pynchon. She was Pynchon's second *Istalena*; the first, designed by Cap'n Nat, was a 62-foot LWL cutter built in 1906.

His 1928 *Istalena* was a massive, yet slender, double-ender that was built at the South Shop of the HMC yard. The contract price was for $50,000, a sum equal to more than $530,000 today. It was very nearly the last opportunity Pynchon would have to buy such a boat; head of one of the nation's largest brokerage firms, Pynchon & Co., with offices in the United States, England, and France, his company would be one of the many victims of the Great Depression, going into receivership in 1931.

The sloop-rigged (with 3,200 square feet of sail) *Istalena* (the name is an Indian word for "water lily") had a full 33 feet of overhang, measuring just 54 feet on the waterline, with a beam of 14 feet, 6 inches and a draft of 10 feet, 5 inches. Among the design and construction tweaks L. Francis employed was the use of the keel as a structural member. He specified that a larger than usual amount of antimony be added to the lead, making it hard enough that contemporary observers reported the lead almost gave out with a ringing sound when struck. Despite this added hardness, the keel was still capable of being milled using standard cutting tools, and the keel was fastened to the hull with a rabbet cut along its length. The new alloy also took bolts and fittings with greater security.

In order to balance the boat fore and aft after launching, or to change the amount of ballast for fine-tuning, the keel had several large cone-shaped cavities cast in it. Into these holes extra lead plugs could be placed (or removed) without having to take the boat out of the water or, as had been done in other boats, removing the keel entirely. When finally launched, *Istalena* had a displacement of 93,400 pounds.

Istalena's racing career began in 1929 with a second-place finish (by 16 seconds) for the King's Cup race in August 1929 and was fifth of nine boats for the New York Yacht Club Cup a few days later.

Istalena (and indeed the entire M-class) came about when the NYYC began to look for a boat to replace the aging fleet of NYYC 50s, and selected the Universal Rule M-class, sufficiently close to the 12 Meter class that, in 1929, the club's Committee on Racing Appeals decided that the two classes would race boat-for-boat.

This proved a boost for the M-class boats, and immediately upon this ruling Harold Vanderbilt commissioned Burgess to design the M-class *Prestige* and Winthrop Aldrich (elected commodore of the NYYC in 1931) commissioned Charles Mower to design *Windward*. Other club members revamped their long-in-the-tooth 50s to compete against the M-class, with Clinton Crane being the designer of choice for that task. By 1927, there was an active fleet of M-class boats rounding marks in NYYC races.

Istalena was commissioned, designed to the maximum length allowed by the class, and built to win. With all her innovations, it took Pynchon, often accompanied by his son George Jr., a season to get his new boat into shape, but she soon came to dominate the class. In 1931, she won the Astor Cup, but with Chandler Hovey at the helm after chartering the boat from Pynchon, who was almost certainly having trouble financing a racing season at that time. L. Francis brokered the charter and eventual sale of the boat.

The M-class boats had a rather short racing history, the result of an international ratings conference held at the NYYC in 1931 that required classes J, K, and L to conform to an agreed-upon international rule (not the International Rule, it should be noted), leaving out the M-class boats. What the ratings conference began the Great Depression finished, with the construction of new M-class boats virtually ceasing.

In 1927, L. Francis was occasionally busy redesigning rigs for existing boats, and when rerigging the R-class *Gypsy* (not his design), he put an overlapping jib on it, thereby creating what would soon develop into the Genoa. In later years, he was to forcefully condemn this arrangement, calling it a rating-based rig that was clumsy to use.

L. Francis was actively engaged in designing meter-boats and R- and Q-class boats. Between 1923 and 1929 he designed seven notable vessels, beginning with the R-class *Jipsey*, in 1923, followed by the above-mentioned R-class boats *Yankee* and *Live Yankee*, in 1925 and 1927, respectively. In 1928, he produced the radically innovative 6 Meter *Wasp* (designed for W. A. W. Stewart and built at the Lawley yard), the Q-class *Nor'Easter V* (also built at Lawley and still sailing on Flathead Lake, Montana; she was designed for Grafton Smith, who asked for a boat with a short waterline that worked best in light weather), the Q-class *Questa*, also still sailing in Montana, and the R-class *Bonnie Lassie*. All these boats were distinguished by their very high ballast ratios, as high as 76 percent in *Bonnie Lassie*. These high ballast ratios were done in the press of competition and ratings; it was a practice, much like the large overlapping headsails, which L. Francis did not personally favor, saying in a letter to his father, "I am trying to stop," and that better design would obviate the advantages, as long as the rules equally restricted all designers.

Cap'n Nat, who distrusted "modern science" in favor of judgment and high-quality materials, replied that there was "nothing really new in the, what you call modern and scientific construction," and that good construction with high-grade material was the answer.

In a few years L. Francis was doing sufficiently well that he began to hire help, both designers and draftsmen. Norman L. Skene went to work for him in 1926, and several other designers/draftsmen came and went, including Fred Goeller and Fenwick Williams; there was something of a revolving door for draftsmen at the Herreshoff studio. In 1928, L. Francis hired designer Samuel Brown, who worked on, among other things, a 32-foot LWL cruising vessel. Brown was hired about the time Skene left; Skene died in a canoeing accident a few years later, ending a career that was most notable for his 1904 book, *Elements of Yacht Design*. L. Francis' relationship with Skene was of long standing, as they both worked as draftsmen with Burgess, Swasey & Paine.

During the early years in Marblehead, L. Francis' work was mostly centered around racing boats, as that was where most of the money was, and in a 1927 letter to his father he called cruising boats "hacks and push-waters and lightships," this despite his problems reconciling good design with ratings rules and design committees.

Carl W. Haffenreffer accepting the Insurance Underwriters Safety Award in April 1944.
Herreshoff Museum

The 12-meter *Mitena*, seen here on trials in 1935, was a 72-foot LOA double-ender. Beautiful to look at, she was disappointing as a racer. *Herreshoff Museum*

L. Francis' one experience with America's Cup boats began with a meeting he had with Pynchon and Paul Hammond in 1929. Cap'n Nat was not initially in favor of his son becoming involved with a Cup syndicate, except that it would give him valuable experience in designing big boats. He knew what an all-consuming job it would become and advised that it would take up "most of your time . . . next summer."

L. Francis was not deterred, however, and upon signing the contract on October 7, 1929, began to work on design number 44, the boat that would become *Whirlwind*, one of four J-class boats built for the 1930 challenge. The challenge was once again by Sir Thomas Lipton, once again with a *Shamrock*, this one *Shamrock V*, designed by Charles Nicholson.

When L. Francis began the design for his Cup J-class boat, he began to draw a boat based on *Istalena*, enlarging her to the J-class limit on waterline of 86 feet. He had just started when, in another conference with Hammond and Pynchon, this time in New York City, he was persuaded (because they were, after all, paying the bill), to model the design more on the NYYC 50. This was, as he stated later, a decision he agreed to "most unfortunately," but the vote was two to one. *Istalena* was by far the better boat, a fact borne out by the boat's racing success, but he agreed to model their boat, at least in its wide after

body and sharp stern, according to their desires. "Hammond, in his usual way, wanted everything changed from whatever arrangement had been made," complained L. Francis in a 1935 letter to British designer Uffa Fox.

US 3, the sail number assigned to the yet-unnamed boat, was the last of the four Js ordered in 1929, and there were not enough boatbuilders capable of working with metal to simultaneously build four metal J-class yachts, so the decision was made to build a composite boat, with steel frames and wood planking. Carl Haffenreffer expressed a desire to build the boat at HMC, and Cap'n Nat said he was "equally anxious [that the boat be built there] and hope it can be brought about."

The Lawley and Son Corporation boatyard in Neponset, near Boston, was instead chosen, which was just as well for Haffenreffer, since his yard was building both Clinton Crane's *Weetamoe* and W. Starling Burgess' *Enterprise*.

L. Francis' troubles with the Cup boat project, which started with the owners wanting to be designers, continued with the Lloyd's inspector, despite the American Bureau of Shipping already approving the boat's design. According to the scantling rules of the time, a composite boat of that size required steel plates over a wood keel, which ruled out bronze keel bolts for reasons of electrolysis. L. Francis thus went with a bronze keel plate, after examining various bronze alloys in consultation with two metallurgists that the American Brass Company provided. The choice was for Everdur, a silicon bronze composite, and when the Lloyd's inspector saw this and the cast bronze keel plate, he condemned it, forcing L. Francis to scrap the existing keel plate and make one of manganese bronze, incurring both cost and delay.

This was yet another decision on the boat that the designer was unhappy about. Manganese bronze is more ductile and often has a small amount of iron in it, while bronze, being stiffer, was exactly what L. Francis wanted in this vital structural component. It was, he said, "plain that the inspector had been instructed to hamstring this yacht."

His boat was designed with much of her ballast inside, this decision being made because he worried that the ways at Lawley's yard were not strong enough to hold the entire weight of a boat with external, i.e., keel, ballast. There were initial problems with the ballast. When the boat was launched, she sat 10 inches at the stern and 18 inches high at the bow. L. Francis had been worried about this because of "the many additions Lloyd's required to the framing," he later wrote. He added some 20 tons more lead in her, bringing the ballast up to the amount used in the other Cup boats being built.

Pynchon's growing financial troubles forced him to sell out his share in the syndicate, the shares going to people L. Francis did not know and whom he "had not heard of in yachting." He was not made aware of this change until it was a fait accompli, and it was the new owner who chose the name, *Whirlwind*, another item in the boat's design process with which he did not agree, calling the name "rather unfortunate."

Labor problems were the next difficulty. The Frank Paine–designed *Yankee*, the fourth J-class Cup boat, was being built next to *Whirlwind*. Because the drawings for *Whirlwind* were done earlier, she was set up closer to the water, as she was started first. When *Whirlwind* was nearly done, her workers walked out on strike, while work continued on *Yankee*, pushing aside *Whirlwind*. This resulted in *Yankee* being finished first; the final work on *Whirlwind* was done so hastily that the waterline was not properly painted.

There were also contract problems, not all of which were immediately evident. L. Francis

Harold S. Vanderbilt at the helm of *Enterprise*, probably during the 1930 Cup season.
Mariners Museum

had a fixed-price contract, awarding him $20,000 for the complete package, including travel, expenses, materials, and overhead. Today, that would be nearly $215,000. Lawley's contract allowed them to add 20 percent to the cost for overhead and another 10 percent for profit, with the total sum to not exceed $250,000, nearly $2.7 million today. Lawley's bill came under scrutiny after World War II when Lawley's books were examined in the course of liquidating the business. An overcharge of some $20,000 was revealed, and, nearly 10 years after the account padding occurred, the syndicate members were reimbursed the overcharge.

Money didn't appear to be a problem with the syndicate, though. With the construction of *Whirlwind* underway, they ordered a towboat,

Twister, design number 45, a 55-foot towboat with two 100-horsepower engines that cost over $12,000 each, nearly $312,000 today. *Twister* was built on the same molds as his *Walrus*, design number 19, an auxiliary ketch built for Charles Welch at Lawley's yard a few months earlier, but *Twister* was built without masts and 5 feet longer. Hammond had seen Welch's boat, which had two six-cylinder, 60-horsepower Lathrop engines and admired it, but wanted a better and bigger version.

The syndicate next chartered a three-masted schooner (L. Francis called it a "lumber schooner") as a tender. They then "filled her up with all sorts of nautical hardware, none of which could have been used on or in tending a racer of any size," he later wrote.

Landon K. Thorne headed the syndicate, and was also, at least according to the contract, the skipper. Thorne, a millionaire banker and philanthropist, was the brother-in-law of Alfred L. Loomis (also a member of the Thorne syndicate), an investment banker who had the foresight to sell his holdings just before the crash of 1929 and a physicist who invented LORAN. He was the founder of Tuxedo Park Loomis Laboratory, which employed such notable physicists as Albert Einstein, Neils Bohr, and Werner Heisenberg.

It was an illustrious syndicate. Other members were Marshall Field III, bond broker, philanthropist, and founder of the *Chicago Sun* newspaper, and 1912 Nobel laureate Elihu Root, international lawyer, ex-senator, and cabinet member under presidents McKinley and Theodore Roosevelt.

Thorne's health precluded his actually skippering the boat, and Hammond took over for the starts and mark rounding, with the principal owner, who, according to L. Francis "never had sailed boats, as far as I can make out, of over about a ton displacement, or had any real experience in racing," steering the rest of the time.

Whirlwind was the biggest of the five Cup boats, including *Shamrock V*, in every measurement but sail area, and all the boats were built to "max out" the rating rule, since this Cup race was to be sailed without handicaps. She measured 130 feet overall, with an 86-foot waterline. The 158-ton boat carried 7,550 square feet of sails, and here another problem surfaced. With the Depression hitting sail lofts as hard as it hit sailboat owners, the Ratsey sail loft on City Island, New York, was the only loft in the country that was capable of making J-class sails.

The *Enterprise* syndicate, headed by Harold S. Vanderbilt, was first in line at Ratsey's and

no sooner had the work been completed than the loft was condemned by the fire inspectors. Thorne knew the right people, however, and things were smoothed over sufficiently to allow Ratsey's sail makers to get back to work. And then the troubles with the sails began.

L. Francis had designed the mainsail head-board to incorporate a sheave for the halyard, something he had been doing for three years on his larger boats. Besides making life easier for the deck crew, there was a ratings advan-tage, since under the Universal Rule the main-sail hoist is measured at the highest point of attachment for the halyard, thus giving "free" sail area to anything above the sheave. The headboards were duly made up by Lawley but Ratsey refused to install them.

Whirlwind's original sail plan, two headsails with parallel luffs, was only used in the first race, during which the clew outhaul pennant broke. As a result, the afterguard dictated that *Whirlwind* be rigged with three headsails, even though the failed part was on the mainsail. The rest of the J-class fleet all had triple headsails, but, as L. Francis pointed out, they were designed for that rig. His boat had been designed for the greater sail area that a twin headsail rig afforded and the change in sail bal-ance soon required a trip to a City Island boat-yard where the entire rig was moved forward 6 feet. It is significant that eventually the rest of the J-class changed their rig to twin headsails.

If the boat seemed to steer hard, L. Francis attributed it to two things, apart from the crew, whose sailing skills L. Francis found question-able, at best. The first was that the boat was sharper in the bow than designed, due to a mistake by the loftsman at Lawley.

More serious was the problem with her mahogany rudder, built just as specified but which floated, thus feeding back erroneous information to the helmsman when the boat was heeled. The boat was fitted with a "reversible" steering mechanism, that is, one that could be turned by the rudder, unlike a non-reversible steering mechanism such as a worm gear in which power can only flow one way.

With all this rig changing and mast mov-ing, the syndicate hired Burgess to measure the sails and hull to determine if the boat was properly balanced. When Crane learned of this, he ventured to L. Francis that this was the greatest insult in the field of yacht design he had ever heard of.

Burgess reported back that the balance was the same as on his boat, *Enterprise*. For his part, L. Francis was not surprised that the balance was the same, because in the years the two of them had worked together they often discussed the relation between the driving force of the sails (the so-called "cen-ter of effort") and the resistance of hulls (the "center of lateral resistance") to sliding off to leeward. As for the insult, it didn't exist in

North Star is a Herreshoff
Mobjack design. The
original design of this
45-foot ketch dates back
to 1935. *Cory Silken*

L. Francis' mind because he and Burgess were the best of friends.

During the boat's series of races to select the Cup defender, L. Francis, who was not pleased with the boat's performance, was invited aboard to race against *Weetamoe* off Newport. After the start and upon being given the helm, he saw the headsails were improperly trimmed and went forward. While there, he related that "the owner and captain came up to me and said in rather cross voices, 'You can't do that.' There was nothing for the designer to do but go below which I did."

Whether *Whirlwind* was actually the slowest, or just sailed the slowest, she only won one of her round of elimination races. It seemed to sour L. Francis on designing boats for committees, and after 1930 he gradually turned to designing boats more suited for cruising.

There were still some racing boats to be designed, though. Always a fan of the meter-boats, his Buzzards Bay one-design boats, design number 52, were built to compete in the 30-square-meter class. In 1931, the price of one built at Lawley was $3,000, $36,000 today, with that price predicated on a fleet of 10 being built. Lawley was given the exclusive right to build the boats, and L. Francis was to receive a commission of 2 1/2 percent of the boat's cost.

The last racing double-ender, in fact, the last big boat designed as a racer, was *Mitena*, design number 62, a 12 Meter done for William J. Strawbridge in 1935. The boat was built at the Herreshoff yard, design number 1275, on a cost-plus contract, with a final price of $50,000, nearly $671,000 today. The name is an Indian word meaning "new moon," and it was Strawbridge's intention to have a boat that would be competitive in the class, which was then being discussed, mostly by the British, as an alternative to the J-class boats for international (which is to say, America's Cup) competition. The NYYC agreed that times were indeed tough, but wanted to continue racing the biggest boats allowed under the Deed of Gift, which meant the J-class.

Mitena was the occasion of yet another fracas with the Lloyd's inspector during construction. Because of this encounter, the boat was built heavier than L. Francis had intended, which resulted in reducing the ballast so that the displacement would remain the same. With the ballast ratio reduced to less than 52 percent, she could not stand up to her sail and was, by any standards, a failure on the race course. "Failure," at least as regards racing sailboats, is a relative term: it only means the boat was not the class champion. She was probably the prettiest boat in the fleet, which at the time mostly consisted of Burgess-designed 12 Meters built at the German yard of Abeking & Rasmussen, and Crane's *Seven Seas*, built for Van S. Merle-Smith and launched earlier the same year as *Mitena*, but she was also one of the slowest.

The same year that *Whirlwind* was discouraging the Thorne syndicate, Hammond took time away from his duties with the boat to commission *Landfall*, design number 49, a 71-foot ketch that was built by Abeking & Rasmussen. Hammond wanted a boat for the 1931 transatlantic race, the first since the 1928

Spanish race. The Cruising Club of America and the Royal Ocean Racing Club sponsored the race, whose course went from Newport, Rhode Island, to Plymouth, England.

Hammond had won the 1928 race on *Niña*, and hoped to repeat the performance. *Landfall* was the scratch boat and finished second to Olin Stephen's *Dorade*, and sixth of the 10-boat fleet on corrected time. *Landfall* was a racing boat, but was designed with fewer compromises to ratings. Perhaps the most significant alteration was to the stern. L. Francis had drawn a gracefully overhanging stern that added nearly 5 feet to the length, but chopped it off for the sake of ratings. As a result of this, possibly because of it, *Landfall* had a transom-hung rudder and a tiller nearly 5 feet long, extending to within 20 inches of the mizzen-mast. The "missing" length was compensated for by a bumpkin 30 inches long, to which was sheeted the mizzen. Running backstays for the mizzen were cleated to the stern quarter.

Landfall carried 3,004 rated square feet of sail, with berths for 18 crewmembers, including a paid captain, Roger Williams. With a removable steering wheel and a seat in the deckhouse, the helmsman had some respite from the weather. She measured 71 feet, 1 1/2 inches overall, with a waterline of 59 feet, 11 inches, beam of 18 feet, and drew 10 feet, 10 inches. The hull flared slightly from the waterline, where the beam was 16 feet, 4 inches, with a fine bow entry that didn't begin to flare until nearly the waterline.

With the exception of her rather ungainly deckhouse, mercilessly, purposefully square, she was a beautiful, ocean-going racing cruiser. The prop was offset to starboard, giving a clean flow to the rudder.

Landfall's fate was less clean. Moored up a river along the Spanish Riviera during World War II, she was mined and sunk by the German army, along with the rest of the boats in the harbor.

The next year, 1931, L. Francis began to truly hit his stride in the designing of boats that were as lovely as they were fast. *Tioga*, design number 50, was designed for Waldo H. Brown, a noted aviator (the World War I Navy aviation veteran died in 1939 piloting a U.S. Navy aircraft during the commissioning ceremony for the aircraft carrier USS *Wasp*). Brown had much input in the design, drawing his inspiration for the boat from a pilot schooner his family owned. L. Francis refined

and developed Brown's thoughts and designed her "for pleasure sailing and to drive efficiently under power," in his words. Typical of L. Francis, the boat had an offset prop, this one to port, powered by a Gray 430 producing 75 horsepower at 1,200 rpm.

Tioga was a centerboard ketch, measuring 57 feet, 6 inches overall, with a 50-foot waterline and a beam of 13 feet, 4 inches. With the board up she drew 4 feet, 7 inches and 9 feet with it down. She had a displacement of 49,460 pounds, including a lead keel of 14,300 pounds, and it was all driven with a sail area of 1,324 square feet.

Tioga had a sister ship, the *Bounty*, design number 58, virtually identical except for the fixed keel, giving a draft of 6 feet, 6 inches and a displacement of 50,960 pounds, with the added displacement almost entirely due to the fixed keel, which was some 1,500 pounds heavier. The sail area was increased to 1,519 feet by virtue of a slightly taller rig, with the mainmast 7 feet taller and the mizzen 5 feet. *Bounty*, the flagship of the Eastern Yacht Club, was designed for Edward Dane and built in 1933 at the Britt Brothers yard.

Bounty wasn't at her best as a racer. She was oversparred for heavy weather and Dane wasn't much for salt-in-your-face racing anyway. Once, a competitor passed *Bounty* at noon because Dane was being served lunch on deck, on a table set with linen and silver, her sails reefed down to provide a genteel platform for alfresco dining.

In 1935, L. Francis had a banner year. One of his best boats, *Mobjack*, design number 63, was also the most popular boat he had ever designed. By 1967, he had sold over 150 sets of plans, at $75 each, for the 45-foot ketch, with more than 200 boats built. She was named for Mobjack Bay, Virginia, where the owner of hull number one, George Upton, had a large estate. Upton at one time was a neighbor of Charles Welch, who commissioned the 68-foot motorsailer *Albatross*, design number 51, but never had it built.

The popularity of *Mobjack* prompted *The Rudder* to publish the plans in March 1947, 12 years after hull number one was built by George Gulliford of Saugus, Massachusetts, "an inexpensive yard," according to L. Francis, which charged just $12,000 ($161,000 today) for the boat. The designer was, at times, dismissive of the qualities of the boat, saying her chief merit was being cheap and easy to build. He would later recommend people consider *Golden Ball*, design number 104, a 46-foot leeboard ketch, which he said was "a superior boat."

Upton had two very tall sons, so the boat was designed with 6 feet, 4 inches of headroom, an arrangement L. Francis conceded was "highly unusual." The layout was also unusual for the day, with the head and galley amidships and a double stateroom forward. The prop was offset to starboard, which was not unusual. *Mobjack* measured 45 feet, 3 inches overall, 38 feet, 9 inches on the waterline with a beam of 12 feet, 6 inches and a minimal draft of just 3 feet, to make her suitable for the waters of Chesapeake Bay. The shallow draft required a fairly high ballast ratio of 41 percent of the 38,600-pound displacement, with 10,200 pounds in the keel and another 6,000 pounds of internal ballast. Total sail area was 1,060 square feet. As designed, *Mobjack* had a tiller, but after sailing the boat for a few days, the owner insisted on a wheel, which the builder installed. For his taste, L. Francis has said he "certainly would not want to use a steering wheel on a boat much less than 45 feet long."

The boat that really distinguished 1935, though, was the big ketch *Tioga II*, design number 66 (Iroquois for "swift current"). *Tioga II* was commissioned by Harry E. Noyes of Marblehead, and it is safe to say he and L. Francis had a rocky relationship, with what has been called "violent quarrels" punctuating the whole design process. It was bad enough that, soon after, L. Francis laid off his entire staff and virtually quit accepting commissions for large yachts.

Built at the Quincy Adams Yacht Yard in 1936, *Tioga II* measured 71 feet overall, 64 feet on the waterline with a beam of 16 feet and drew 7 feet, 9 inches. Built of wood, she displaced 108,000 pounds with a 37,750-pound lead keel and carried 2,800 square feet of sail, but, though her owner's intended use was for daysailing and coastal cruising, she was an outstanding ocean racer. L. Francis put his heart and soul into the graceful lines and elegant sheer. He said she was designed above water to be "similar to some of the fast yachts of 75 years ago with the grace and seaworthiness of this type before measurement rules showed their effects," while below the waterline the cutaway forefoot and reduced deadwood aft gave her the ability to turn smartly. It is worth noting that Frederick Goeller, one of L. Francis'

Opposite: *Honalee* is a Herreshoff Rozinante ketch of 42 feet. She sails on San Francisco Bay. *Mariah's Eyes Photography*

draftsmen, did much of the detail shaping work on *Tioga II*, presumably under the oversight of his boss.

With these seemingly contradictory design intentions between owner and designer, the contretemps they had were perhaps inevitable. As it turned out, Noyes did race her. She went out and finished first in 24 of her first 37 races. She sailed the 171 miles from New London, Connecticut, to Marblehead, Massachusetts, in 18 hours, cutting nearly two hours off the 1911 record set by the 136-foot schooner *Elena*. In 1941, she did the 184-mile Miami-Nassau race in 19 hours, 36 minutes, thus beginning a 25-year period in which she literally dominated the races held by the Southern Ocean Racing Circuit.

She was "drafted" into service by the Coast Guard during World War II. She served as a submarine picket patrol boat on the East Coast, surviving to return to racing after being purchased and renamed *Ticonderoga* (also Iroquois, for "between the lakes") by Alan P. Carlisle in 1946. At one time she held more than 30 course records and was actively raced until 1968 under the ownership of Robert Johnson. Her most famous victory in those years was probably her record-setting first-overall-finish in the 1965 Transpac race. Yes, she was a racer, but also elegant, in the finest sense of the word. In 1968, she was converted for use as a luxury charter boat.

L. Francis was a slow, exceedingly meticulous designer. His output at Marblehead, just 107 designs in all, would have been even less without the assistance of his staff, all capable designers in their own right. *Persephone*, design number 69, was the biggest boat he designed and drew singlehanded, creating it in the years 1936 to 1937, after he dismissed his staff. The racing yawl was designed for Strawbridge, owner of *Mitena*, and adhered, possibly more than L. Francis would have liked, to the Cruising Club of America's ratings system. This produced slender, deep-drafted boats, not in itself a bad thing for speed, and *Persephone* (the name is from Greek mythology; she was Pluto's wife, queen of Hades) was a very successful racer. She measured 55 feet on deck, 40 feet on the waterline, 12 feet, 7 inches beam and drew 7 feet, 9 inches. She was double-planked, with the two layers set in shellac.

The mizzen sail was tiny, just 135 square feet, and was probably only there as a nod to the CCA, much like another yawl of that period, Olin Stephens' *Stormy Weather*. There was no triatic stay; instead, the permanent backstay for the mainmast was rigged to a jumper strut on the mizzen. Total sail area was 1,421 square feet. In the interests of speed, a 16-inch feathering prop was offset to starboard.

The decks were clear and uncluttered, with a very low cabintop, saloon skylight, and forward hatch, allowing ample room for the racing crew to work.

Belowdecks, the minimal head for the crew was tucked up in the forepeak, sharing the space with two foldup pipe berths and the galley. The two aft berths were simple, laced canvas affairs. Another head was amidships to port, with a small washbasin that drained into the toilet. This was a racing boat without even a nod to luxury.

After *Persephone*, L. Francis busied himself with a number of small boat designs. There were some notable exceptions, one being a 110-foot version of *Tioga II* done in 1957 (not given a design number on the drawings), a three-masted schooner that was never built.

One of his best-loved boats was *Prudence*, design number 71, done in 1937. He said this trim little sloop (22 feet, 9 inches overall and displacing 6,888 pounds with a 45 percent ballast ratio) possessed only two disadvantages: "People will constantly want to borrow her and she is apt to be stolen." *Prudence* exemplified the simple cruising style he came to espouse more vocally as he grew older and shed the clients who wanted boats contrary to that philosophy. There were several built, the first completed at the Quincy Adams yard in 1942.

The schooner *Mistral*, design number 73, was built in 1937 for Theodore Little, who took her around the world. On her, L. Francis was able to finally use the headboards with integral sheaves he had tried to install on *Whirlwind*, and they performed flawlessly for the entire voyage. *Mistral* carried a gaff foresail and a Bermudan main. A vang, attached to the mainmast, was used to reduce the twist in the tall, narrow gaff foresail. The total sail area was 1,972 square feet. She measured 63 feet, 6 inches overall, 54 feet, 9 inches on the waterline and had a beam of 15 feet. The draft was moderate for a boat of her size, only 6 feet, 3 inches.

L. Francis probably agreed to design this boat because he was given the freedom to draw her as he saw fit. Her graceful clipper bow, traditional plank-on-frame construction, and

straightforward yet gracious design made her as attractive for him to design as she was to look at.

In 1940 came *Solitair*, design number 76, an enlarged *Prudence*, stretched out to 28 feet, 3 inches. She displaced roughly 12,000 pounds; the rest of the measurements are LWL, 23 feet, 3 inches; beam, 9 feet, 3 inches; and draft, 4 feet, 10 inches, with a total sail area of 446 square feet. She was built for a Mr. Sawyer and later sold and renamed *Normerry*.

The Rudder magazine was probably the most influential and important yachting magazine of its day. It was through the efforts of its early editor Thomas Fleming Day that ocean racing in small boats was seen to be possible. In 1942, Boris Lauer-Leonardi became editor of *The Rudder*, and he could hardly have taken the job at a worse time. The country had just entered a war that had been raging since 1939 and people had other things on their minds besides sailboats. Or reading about them. With circulation dropping, Boris began to seek ways of maintaining interest in the subject, perhaps as a welcome diversion from the tiresome, daily reports of the war. He contacted L. Francis and suggested he write an article or two on building a small boat, one that soldiers and civilians could dream about until the war was over.

Although L. Francis had done some magazine writing already, this was the beginning of a steady flow of editorial material that would continue until the 1960s. It started with a series of 11 monthly installments on building the H-28 ketch, design number 80. The pace was just about right for L. Francis, who covered subjects from nautical flags to how-to-build stories to what could best be termed sea stories. His unique philosophy was evident in all his writings, and as he continued to write into his old age his readers seemed to take delight in his increasing curmudgeonry.

The H-28 series was the salvation of the magazine. The boat was inspiration for hundreds of home building projects and many built at yards. She measured just 28 feet overall, with a waterline of 23 feet, 6 inches; a beam of 8 feet, 9 inches; and a draft of 3 feet, 6 inches. She displaced 9,500 pounds, with a ballast ratio of 31 percent and carried 343 square feet of sail. No one would accuse the H-28 of being revolutionary or even remarkable, except for the philosophy that went with the boat. As defined by L. Francis, the sailboat, in particular the H-28, was a lifestyle, although he would never have used the word. It offered the opportunity for contemplation, recreation, and character building. Literally

hundreds of H-28 plans were sold, with L. Francis receiving $10 of the $15 *The Rudder* charged for them.

The builders often made changes in the boat, nearly all of which, when L. Francis was consulted about them, he disapproved of. The boat was a phenomenon, and its success provided the impetus for more boat plans in *The Rudder*.

He still designed boats for individual clients, such as *Quiet Tune*, design number 82, done for Edwin H. Hill in 1944. Using the same sail plan as the H-28, *Quiet Tune* was a ketch measuring 29 feet, 6 inches overall and 25 feet on the waterline. She was slimmer than her smaller sister, at 7 feet, 10 inches, but drew 4 feet, 6 inches. Lighter, more easily driven, with a higher ballast ratio of 43.25 percent, *Quiet Tune* displaced 8,100 pounds.

The H-14 dinghy, design number 84, occupied two issues of the magazine in 1944, a hard-chined 14-foot daggerboard dinghy with a gunter main that promised to provide everything from relaxation for weary workers to lessons in maturation for young men.

In January 1945, he began the lengthy series of articles, 21 in all, on *Marco Polo*, design number 85, along with its own 11-foot, 6-inch lugsail tender, equipped with leeboards. *Marco Polo* was a three-masted schooner that was really a motorsailer, an ocean passage-maker that, with a big, reliable engine, could turn in 120- to 200-mile days with a crew of four or five. "With the proper engine one can maintain a speed of 240 miles in 24 hours," he

promised in one of the articles. For the time, it was revolutionary in concept, and, as the designer had not actually sailed in such a boat, some of the ideas didn't work out as planned once the boat was built.

The boat was indeed fast. With a displacement of 93,500 pounds and a ballast ratio of 37 percent, she was sufficiently stable, and the hull, long and lean, measuring 55 feet LOA; 48 feet, 9 inches LWL with a beam of just 10 feet; and a long fin-type keel drawing 5 feet, 6 inches, was easily driven.

By 1967, there were 20 of them built, and all of them incorporated changes in the rigging. There were two or three rigged as sloops and one as a powerboat.

In 1945, L. Francis moved from his house on Lee Street to Castle Brattahlid at Crocker Park, also in Marblehead, with a view of the harbor. More commonly known as "the Castle," the large house was perfectly named, with crenellated parapets and thick stone walls. He set up his lathe under a crystal chandelier, and lived in rooms whose décor was planned as carefully as his boats. Each room had at least one object of artistic merit, something of such exquisite taste or so unique that one's eyes were drawn to it. Although he regularly complained to Boris that he needed his editorial payment to prevent poverty, he had investments made upon the advice of some of his clients, whose ability to make money was unquestioned. He had good taste in automobiles, and could often be seen driving his two-seater Ferrari.

Nereia, design number 87, was the next major project, taking 15 issues to complete, beginning in March 1947. She was a 36-foot ketch, the name taken from Greek mythology, Nereia being one of the daughters of Nereus, the sea god (and sister-in-law to Neptune). The boat can be most easily described as the very big sister ship to the H-28, just as *Prudence* was a smaller version, and *Mobjack* was a close cousin. Letters to L. Francis from *Rudder* readers were always asking for an H-28 that was a bit bigger (or, more rarely, smaller) and *Nereia* was an effort to satisfy the eternal desire among sailors for a boat that is just a little bit bigger.

At 36 feet overall, she was that, displacing 24,000 pounds with a 50 percent ballast ratio. She had a waterline of 31 feet, 9 inches, and more beam than *Marco Polo*, at 11 feet. The full keel, with no cutaway and a slight drag to the lower profile, drew 5 feet, 3 inches. She carried a sail area of 673 square feet, proportionally more than on the H-28.

Design number 88, *Meadowlark*, begun in 1948, was a 33-foot sharpie, drawing just 15 inches with leeboards, the first large boat by a major designer to use them in this country. Except for *Marco Polo's* tender, he had little practical experience with this sort of boat, and as it turned out, the leeboards were far too small. Patient builders, with the courage to change L. Francis' design, eventually learned that if they made them 8 feet, 10 inches long, rather than the specified 5 feet, 5 3/4 inches, the boat would actually sail, and pretty well besides. When he learned of this, he made a note to that effect in subsequent plans, but didn't change the drawings.

Meadowlark had a lead keel, of sorts, weighing 2,500 pounds, 24 inches long in 6-inch sections, bolted to the frames and flush with the deadwood. She carried an additional 1,000 pounds of inside ballast, for an all-up displacement of 8,000 pounds.

Ketch-rigged, with gaff sails that featured very short gaffs, it was a rig chosen for ease of handling and efficiency off the wind. Of *Meadowlark*, L. Francis wrote that she "is a type that will give much pleasure, and perhaps is the cheapest small moving home which combines safety and some speed." He went on to opine that she could be lived aboard year-round "any-where south of the Mason-Dixon line . . . and would be cheap to service and keep up."

Araminta, design number 89 (not featured in *The Rudder*), was built for Edwin M. Hill and designed during the period 1948 to 1954. In letters, L. Francis intimated that she was his favorite design, the smallest clipper-bowed ketch he designed, at 33 feet overall, and in many ways very similar (but 3 feet, 3 inches longer) to *Quiet Tune*, except for the bow. On her he again used the rabbeted lead keel assembly he used on *Istalena*, and with her increased sail area of 582 square feet, and a displacement of 12,160 pounds, she was a lively performer. The ballast ratio was typically high at 49 percent.

Rozinante, design number 98, was the subject of a 14-page "how to build" article in the May 1961 issue of *The Rudder*. L. Francis, after much etymological discussion, informed the reader that she was a "canoe yawl," a boat designed to "give more lasting pleasure for the money than any other vessel except for a double-paddle canoe," by which he meant a kayak. She had no engine, with the intention of the designer being that she be rowed when necessary. *Rozinante* was a ketch, 28 feet overall, 24 feet on the waterline, with a beam of 6 feet, 4 inches and a full keel with a slightly cutaway forefoot drawing 3 feet, 9 inches. She displaced just over 7,000 pounds, with a stiff 51 percent ballast ratio.

In writing about *Rozinante* L. Francis really hit his stride. Of the low headroom he said that "most of the sailormen I have known sat down when they ate and preferred to lie down when they slept." He took a swipe at the ratings rules, saying they "penalize the speed-giving qualities of a sailboat," and that her style would be in fashion "long after the abortions of the present are forgotten . . . dangerous and expensive rule-cheating wind-bags." He admitted that she might be better with a sliding hatch, but these cost $150 and "I would duck my head many times for that sum."

Below and opposite:

Elsie's wooden interior is as beautifully finished and laid out as her exterior.

Covey Island Boatworks

For a 28-foot boat, the rig is complex, with twin spreaders and a jumper strut on the mainmast, a single spreader on the mizzenmast and a triatic stay that attaches a fifth of the way from the truck of the mizzen. To some tastes, her freeboard may be excessive, but she was the last of *The Rudder's* how-to-build series, perhaps the culmination of L. Francis' philosophy on why we should own and sail a boat: for the respite from a mechanical and all-consuming world, for the personal challenge of meeting the wind and the sea on its own terms.

Golden Ball was another shoal-draft leeboard ketch, built in 1962 for $30,000, which is roughly $182,000 today. She was built for R. P. Gibbs, who already owned a *Meadowlark* but wanted, in the usual manner, something a little bigger. She measured 46 feet, 6 inches overall; 40 feet, 9 inches on the waterline; with a beam of 11 feet and a draft of just 2 feet. She displaced 21,120 pounds, with 4,200 pounds of external ballast and another 4,920 inside, but had a generous 874 square feet of sail area, on two short-gaff sails of the sort used on *Meadowlark*. The leeboards were long, over 13 feet, possibly as a result of the lessons learned from *Meadowlark*, and when not sailing she could motor along powered by two, 25 horsepower engines.

Golden Ball was a boat that L. Francis said he would like to have had when he was younger, as he thought her "one of my best." In previous how-to articles, L. Francis had written detailed instructions on home-building boats like the 55-foot *Marco Polo*. Now, with perhaps the wisdom of having seen how difficult it was for even a professional boatbuilder to execute some of his plans, he suggested that *Golden Ball* was "a rather large boat for one to build in his backyard."

In March 1960, L. Francis did a preliminary design treatment for *Unicorn*, design number 106, for Stanley Woodward. *Unicorn* was a solid, heavy, clipper-bowed ketch with three courses of square sails on the mainmast, in addition to fore-and-aft sails for windward work. The area of the three downwind squaresails, consisting of a main course, topsail, and a triangular raffee, totaled 1,426 square feet, with 2,417 square feet of fore-and-aft sails. She was rigged with a mizzen staysail and a Bermudan mizzen, plus two headsails for windward sailing. This was to be a big boat, displacing 84,860 pounds; 67 feet, 9 inches LOA; 58 feet, 6 inches LWL; and a beam of 6 feet, 3 inches, with a draft of just over 7 feet.

The last boat to come off L. Francis' board was another leeboard ketch, design number 107. She was 38 feet LOA; 33 feet, 3 inches LWL; had a beam of 9 feet, 6 inches; and, with leeboards to keep her pointing in the right direction, only drew 3 feet. Steered with a tiller, carrying 602 square feet of sail on the short-gaff headed sails he favored, with a displacement of 15,600 pounds, she was designed with a ballast ratio of 36 percent. For ultimate maneuverability under power, she had two engines and twin screws. It was also easier to place two small engines in a shallow hull than one large one in the middle of things.

In 1982, L. Francis broke his hip and was admitted to a hospital in Boston, where he died after surgery on December 3, at the age of 82. He was a bachelor his entire life, yet had a fondness for women that was composed of equal parts puzzlement and admiration.

While he is remembered as a yacht designer, and he designed some very successful and innovative racing yachts, it is for his unfailing aesthetic sense that he is best remembered. His yachts were poetry on the water, graceful creatures best made of wood. He had no love for fiberglass, calling it "unlovely" and "frozen snot."

His lifetime output consisted of just 131 designs taken to the point that a boat could be built from the drawings. Of those designs, 107 were done while he resided in Marblehead; just 73 actually became boats.

The year before he died, he designed three *Rozinante* canoe yawls, one to be his personal boat. They were built at the Lee Boat Shop in Rockland, Maine, and are sailing today. He made the hardware for the boats at the Castle, turning them on the same lathe he used to make his famed brass signaling cannons. Ten of them were made to accompany boats he designed and built, and three were especially commissioned by Harry Noyes, owner of *Tioga II*.

L. Francis was a consummate craftsman, building sea chests and cedar buckets for his friends, and was a prolific writer of letters. He answered nearly every letter, even if it was only to tell the writer that he wouldn't build a boat for them or that the boat they were looking for wasn't designed by him. Modest, shy, he never accepted any of the requests to speak in public. "I can not and do not ever speak in public," he replied to one such request. His favored method of communication was the written word, with articles published in *The Rudder*, *Yachting*, *Fore'n Aft*, and, at one time or another, nearly every magazine concerned with things nautical, both in the United States and England.

Although he wrote *History of Yachting*, among other books, he never considered himself a historian, just an amateur writing about a subject to which he literally devoted his entire life and full attention.

The world's seas are prettier places because of his boats. He compared the lines of a boat to music, to sculpture. "Perhaps some have not heard the music or felt the poetry," he wrote, "but it is there just the same."

Index